*"No matter your religion, you will find yourself joyously celebrating the victories of these women."*

—K. Kai Anderson, Ph.D., and Author of
*CRACKED: Why Your Nest Egg is at Risk*

"I finally was able to have some quiet time this afternoon to read the preview book you sent me. I absolutely loved it! I was amazed by the tremendous challenges each woman faced, and how faith, courage, strength, and love have helped them face and overcome their challenges! It is a beautiful book filled with wisdom, hope, and inspiration! I am so glad I was given the opportunity to read it. I have family members and friends who I know would love your book, and I can't wait to tell them about it!"

—Allison O'Brian
Macedon, New York

*"WOW!! LOVE IT!! God's timing is always spot on. Making a cup of tea to sit down and reread it...Congrats!"*

—Vicki Thomlinson, CEO
Curve to Success

Check out
www.GodGaveUsWings.com
Receive Oprah's 10 Success Tips!

GOD GAVE US
# Wings

Praise for

# GOD GAVE US Wings

People are getting inspiration from just a quick preview of the courageous women who tell their stories in God Gave Us Wings.

*"I just finished reading the preview book. WOW! And WONDERFUL! I believe* God Gave Us Wings *is the next* Chicken Soup for the Soul. *May God continue to bless the work of your hands, open more doors of opportunity for you, and increase you in ways you never could have imagined. Thanks for stirring my desire to spread the wings He has given me. Please keep writing. THANKS again. Blessings!"*

—Wilma Hollis, Blogger

Life Speak Living

*"Thanks so very much! In one word, Wow! When you started with Ms. Oprah, I expected to see just the rich, famous, influential. What follows [are] extraordinary stories of "ordinary" women who decided that God gave them wings and that no person nor circumstance could prevent them from flying and achieving all that God had in store for them. Great work, Connie. I'll be waiting for the finished book."*

—James Oloo, Research Coordinator

Gabriel Dumont Institute

*"Awesome Awesome Awesome!!! This book was a tremendous blessing to read. When a person is in need of a Divine Miracle from on high, these stories will encourage and strengthen their prayer life. If anyone has a heart and a relationship with the Lord Jesus Christ, then this book will reach it! Forever remaining in His service."*

—Apostle Katrina M. Walker, Founder & CEO

Christ Covenant Church, International

GOD GAVE US

# Wings

A Journey to Success:
THEIRS, MINE, *and* YOURS

## Connie Rankin

NEW YORK

NASHVILLE • MELBOURNE • VANCOUVER

# GOD GAVE US Wings
## A Journey to Success: THEIRS, MINE, and YOURS

© 2017 Connie Rankin

Published in New York, New York, by Morgan James Publishing. Morgan James is a trademark of Morgan James, LLC. www.MorganJamesPublishing.com

The Morgan James Speakers Group can bring authors to your live event. For more information or to book an event visit The Morgan James Speakers Group at www.TheMorganJamesSpeakersGroup.com.

ISBN 978-1-68350-133-6 paperback
ISBN 978-1-68350-134-3 eBook
ISBN 978-1-68350-135-0 hardcover
Library of Congress Control Number:
2016909950

**Cover Design by:**
Mike Magnan
www.n8marketing.com and
Rachel Lopez
www.r2design.com

**Interior Design by:**
Bonnie Bushman
The Whole Caboodle Graphic Design

In an effort to support local communities, raise awareness and funds, Morgan James Publishing donates a percentage of all book sales for the life of each book to Habitat for Humanity Peninsula and Greater Williamsburg.

Get involved today! Visit
www.MorganJamesBuilds.com

*To my loving husband, Don, my friend and confidant:*

*I find more reasons every day to love you, and I am so blessed to be your wife. Thank you for always believing in me and encouraging me to follow my dreams. You continue to challenge me to be a better person, and you are an excellent example of what a man should be.*

*and*

*To my mother, my protector:*

*The older I get, the more I can appreciate you as a person, mother, and friend. Sadly, I didn't realize how much I would miss you until you were gone. You were always my protector, and I can hear your words echoing in mind, saying "Lordy…Lordy…Lordy!"*

*…shall ye be as the wings of a dove covered with silver, and her feathers with yellow gold."*
—Psalm 68:13 (KJV)

# Table of Contents

# Foreword

How could I say "no" to God?

"I heard your name three times in the middle of the night. God wants you to write the foreword to my book." Those were Connie's words to me. I was honored, flattered, and shocked. This kind of divine serendipity coupled with synchronicity is how she and I formed a friendship after meeting (believe it or not) on Twitter! I am not kidding. In June 2015, my inner voice whispered, "We are spiritually aligned." I found myself typing those words to Connie after reading the preview to *God Gave Us Wings*. I was awestruck by her drive, passion, and heart-aligned intention and determination to tell the spiritually motivating stories that she shares in the book. Trust me—this read will bring you to tears and make you smile, all while inspiring you on your path.

I am a board-certified adult (Emory University residency) and child (UCLA fellowship) psychiatrist with 20 years of clinical experience and have more than 40,000 patient hours of service working with children, teens, and adults. Did you know that the word "psychiatrist" translates in Greek to "Doctor of the Soul"—*psych* (soul) + *iatros* (doctor)? This definition resonates with me, as I believe that reaching our highest soul alignment is a multidimensional path that integrates a spirit, mind, and body approach and includes all paths to well-being. As a doctor, I love it when my patients go from crisis to thriving, which is why I was intrigued by the resiliency and success stories of Connie and the other remarkable women. I wanted more insight into how their hardships, struggles, and other life lessons became victories and triumphs that resulted in their unique thrive stories—so much so that I suggested that Connie and I talk on the phone!

On a two-hour phone call on June 16, 2015, I asked Connie what motivated her to write this book. She said, "I felt empty. Just one year ago, I was so focused on making money in commercial real estate that I missed my 11-year-old grandson's first home run. That was my 'aha moment.'" I inquired about her writing style. Here is what she said: "I am a deep meditator. I get a jolt of information, and if it happens three times, I know it is important, really important. It is my sign from God. I was meditating when the name Oprah came to me." Connie described her divine download as a faith-driven sign that Oprah needed to be a story in this book. I know what you are thinking: of course, it is a good idea to have Oprah in your book, right? That is what I was thinking, too! "This was bigger than Oprah," Connie said. As a doctor, I am a believer in "show me the data" coupled with an intuitive knowing. As I write this, I want all of you to know that I have my notes and observations in a notebook labeled "Connie Rankin"—Connie laughed when I told her this! In bold print, my notes on Connie Rankin say **PASSION + TENACITY + FAITH**.

Connie's passion, tenacity, and faith led her to complete her intention of meeting Oprah. While on the phone, she described gathering in a venue suite with dear friends and praying before meeting her. "I was turning this over to my higher power for wisdom and knowledge," Connie explained. When she told Oprah about her book, her intentions, and her desire to get her blessing for including her story in *God Gave Us Wings*, that moment stood still in time for Connie. "Oprah held both of my hands and said, 'You have my blessing to add my story in your book.' Oprah gave me her blessing!" This level of love, compassion, concern, and reverence was utilized in Connie's approach to interviewing everyone in this book.

Talking on the phone was not enough for Connie. She strongly stated in our conversation, "I am flying to meet you." This is how Connie rolls! Connie flew from Houston to Los Angeles with her closest friends, who I now endearingly call my "HOU-LA Sisters" (in honor of the "Ya-Ya Sisterhood"), for us to meet in person to discuss ways we could combine our collective experience, intellect, and passion for being of service to others.

When she arrived, I asked Connie if I could interview her in greater detail during her visit, as I was intrigued to know more about her story of thriving and how she survived her childhood accident. Connie regressed back in time and experienced emotionally what she did at five years old: "I felt at total peace. I felt at total peace. I knew I was going to die. 'God, I love you. I love my mother, too.' I didn't think my mom would make it without me." She was trembling in my office when she shared her recollections. "Why are you falling, Connie? You can walk," her doctor from Grady Memorial reminded her during intensive physical therapy while she was attempting to walk around a track. I cannot reveal the rest, as it is Connie's story to tell you in the pages ahead. But what I can tell you is that I was inspired by young Connie's ability to let her fear be a vibration of the past and that her faith in God allowed the vibration of love to prevail to this day.

Are you ready to be inspired?

Each inspirational story includes part testimony and part empowerment with vivid recall of each woman's struggle before gaining their life force and aligning with her highest purpose. The ten extraordinary women in *God Gave Us Wings* have called upon their strength, resiliency, love, and faith to overcome incredible odds and to become exemplary role models for their families, communities, and people worldwide.

Sit back, get comfortable, and be ready to be galvanized by the words, thoughts, and love in the following pages.

—Denise McDermott, MD
Board-Certified Adult and Child Psychiatrist
DrDeniseMD.com

# Introduction

Let's pretend you are in dire need of help. Whom would you call on first? The police, family, friends? Do you know their name?

In the Bible, there are hundreds of different names and titles for God, Jesus Christ, and the Holy Spirit. For the purpose of this book, He is referred to solely as God. He was the One most called upon by the women who have shared their amazing journeys in this book.

Some people feel God is dead, and others believe He is alive and well. What is the significant difference? It's faith! If you know God, you know He will carry you under his wings until you are strong enough to fly victoriously to the other side. Ten faith-driven females show by example how you can change your life in any given situation. These women achieved their dreams through faith that carried them through their tumultuous storms to later fly like an eagle.

More than 9 in 10 Americans still say "yes" when asked if they believe in God or a universal spirit. This is down slightly from 92 percent, from Gallup's poll of 70 years ago. The only difference found in 2010 was that the question was expanded to include the universal spirit. The numbers indicate that 80 percent believe in God, 12 percent believe in a universal spirit, 6 percent don't believe, 1 percent are listed as "other," and 1 percent have no opinion. These numbers suggest overwhelmingly that Americans do believe there is a God.

We know God is called by many names, and sometimes the name differs among cultures and peoples. I believe that knowing God has more to do with the heart than with the logical mind. Having faith involves taking a leap without the absolute certainty of where you'll land. Across all religions that have a concept of God, one belief is constant: God is the creator of all things, and if He is the creator, only He is in full control.

Once we accept that we cannot control everything, then we have greater peace in our lives. We can then fully embrace the serenity prayer: "God grant me the serenity to accept the things I cannot change, the courage to change the things I can, and the wisdom to know the difference."

If you are searching for God, talk to people who have a well-rounded relationship with Him. Ask questions like "Why do you believe?" and "Why should I believe?" These types of questions will help you find the answers you may have missed. Try praying for guidance to lead you to the answers you most seek. The Bible emphasizes that God works in mysterious ways, and I believe that it's always in our best interests. Think of God as a teacher, helping us through valuable life lessons, for us to arrive at a solution for ourselves.

What was my solution? I turned my life over to God and began trusting in His wisdom to guide me in my mission to show others by example how they can develop strong wings to carry them through life. I came to realize that God gives us all wings so that we may fly, but like baby chicks, we need encouragement to do so. Sometimes, this encouragement is subtle, as when a mother bird begins removing the soft stuffing in the nest, exposing more of the thorn-like objects to get the chick to eventually jump out and fly.

> *Once upon a time, when women were birds, there was the simple understanding that to sing at dawn and to sing at dusk was to heal the world through joy. The birds still remember what we have forgotten, that the world is meant to be celebrated.*
> —Tempest Williams

The real joy of believing in a higher power like God is that you begin to respond more from love, rather than judgment since we are all children of God. Even though sometimes the most religious can get lost along the way and must pray for guidance.

Have you ever felt lost, empty, and joyless? I did a few years ago, after almost losing my commercial real estate company during the recession. I started acting out of fear instead of faith, which then activated the "not enough syndrome," making me care only about making money. To be frank, the only joy I experienced was in closing sales. Sadly, it wasn't from time spent living in fulfilling relationships with God, family, friends, and community.

One day, out of sheer desperation, I cried out for God to give me back my joy. His answer wasn't what I expected: it was made clear that I had stopped doing what mattered most, and that was living a life based on faith. I was prompted to write a book called *God Gave Us Wings* to empower others to move past their fear into faith. Fast-forward, I met Oprah Winfrey at "The Life You Want" weekend, and she gave me her blessing to include her empowering story in *God Gave Us Wings: A Journey to Success: Theirs, Mine, and Yours.*

Once you've moved past your fear into faith, you will begin to soar on wings like eagles and climb high up above the sky, experiencing such joy and love that it will leave you breathless—and then you will know that there is a God.

*God Gave Us Wings* is a spiritual illustration of success, a nonfiction book that shares the wisdom and experience of 10 amazing women. It features incredible true stories which sometimes begin to spin out of control, from Oprah's personal journey to a wounded soldier's battle to survive.

Their remarkable stories were written as a catalyst to empower female readers and propel them toward success. The women in this book have boldly defined their words for success. Their achievements demonstrate that no matter what your circumstances, you can rise higher than you ever imagined.

If you like Jack Canfield's Chicken Soup for the Soul, then you will love this book.

Get ready to be inspired!

## CHAPTER 1

# The Past Forward

*...The spiritual concepts of our Ancestors gave birth to religious thought...people believe in oneness of the...family through sacred time, which unites the past, the present and the future. Our Ancestors live with us.*

—Marimba Ani

## A QUEEN'S ANCESTRAL PASSAGE

Travel with me on the incredible journey of Oprah Winfrey's ascent to stardom, community conscience, philanthropist, and best friend to the world. It is a story that began many years ago with her second great-grandparents, who used education to achieve equality for all and helped her to clear a pathway to success for future generations.

How much do our ancestors influence the ways our lives unfold? The choices we make? The values that shape us? Any search for a deeper truth should first look backward to see what we might learn from past generations. That certainly is the case with Oprah. Her dramatic family history seems to have left an indelible mark on her psyche. The hopes and dreams of Oprah's ancestors are being played out in her amazing life. The answer to "What do our ancestors mean to our lives?" becomes even more dramatic when we look at the life of the woman sometimes called the "Queen of Queens."

Is it possible for our second great-grandparents to pass along specific traits, such as a love of education or knowledge about how to amass wealth? After reading *Finding Oprah's Roots*, written by Henry Louis Gates Jr., I believe the answer is "yes." These two major motifs have run through Oprah's family story since at least 1860, repeating themselves from generation to generation. From facing and enduring slavery, racism, and poverty to finding the strength to survive the turmoil of sexual abuse, Oprah's story reflects her roots and how she has used them to guide her.

Through DNA testing and historical evidence, it is believed Oprah's maternal ancestors, known as the Kpelle people, came from Liberia. Professors John Thornton and Linda Heywood, along with other historians, think it entirely possible that one of her ancestors was captured and then enslaved during a war or due to marriage-related issues like adultery or being pawned in exchange for a bride price.

More recently, the oldest recorded generation on Oprah's maternal side is represented by her second great-grandparents, Henrietta and Pearce Winters. Both were born slaves in Mississippi around 1849 and 1855 and overcame their humble beginnings, ending up as landowners and helping to start a school. On Oprah's paternal side, we discover her second great-grandparents, Constantine and Violet Winfrey. Constantine was born in 1836 in Georgia, and his wife was born in North Carolina in 1839; they had eight children. Like most slaves at the time, the family's last name probably came from slave owner, Absalom F. Winfrey.

Remarkably, Constantine Winfrey not only taught himself to read and write over just a 10-year period, but he embraced education for the rest of his people. In 1906, he moved an entire schoolhouse to his property to provide an education for the area's black children. That was a tremendous accomplishment, given the racial tensions in post–Civil War Mississippi. Once freed, he could have chosen to lay low and just take care of his immediate family. Instead, he decided to make a difference for all of the children in his community by providing education to show them a path out of the despair of their circumstances.

Several of Oprah's ancestors exhibited this exceptional commitment to education and unusual intellectual ability. Of course, this does not constitute scientific proof of why Oprah is who she is, but it is certainly worth contemplating. Likewise, it may be worth mentioning that not only did Constantine share the benefits of his hard-won literacy with his community, but he also managed to amass 80 acres of land, which supported his family and his philanthropic activities.

The next chapter of Oprah's story belongs to her maternal great-grandmother, Amanda, the mother of Oprah's grandmother, Hattie Mae. Amanda was one of Henrietta and Pearce Winters's five children. Interestingly, according to *Finding Oprah's Roots*, all five attended college. Two became teachers, including Amanda, who taught English. In 1929, Amanda was appointed one of three trustees of Buffalo Rosenwald School—a very rare achievement for a woman of her day, white or black. Her appointment is clear evidence of her high standing and power in the local community and church. Obviously, Amanda was an accomplished woman; she also was one of the organizers of the Methodist Church in Kosciusko, Mississippi.

One looming mystery among the generations, however, is how Hattie Mae Presley, Amanda's daughter and Oprah's grandmother, grew up semi-literate. No clear answers exist, except perhaps that before Amanda married her second husband, Charles Bullock, her life and the lives of her children were very different. According to *Finding Oprah's Roots*, "The 1910 census indicated that Amanda and all her children, including 10-year-old Hattie Mae, were living on a farm working as laborers, and none was attending school. Young Hattie Mae, the census indicates, could read but not write—and it is very likely that her education was over at that point. She would be a laborer for the rest of her days." When Amanda married Charles Bullock, her circumstances improved significantly, but for whatever reason, Hattie Mae seemed to benefit little from her mother's newfound prosperity.

God does not waste any life experiences. Sometimes, he uses the bumpy road of the past to strengthen us to fly over obstacles to reach our brilliant future.

Now, fast-forward to 1953 in the Deep South. Two people meet and ignite a spark that grew a beautiful baby girl into America's first black female billionaire.

## A QUEEN IS BORN

Oprah's mother and military father were impressionable, unmarried, and young—18 and 20 years old, respectively—when they decided to let passion overrule logic under an oak tree. The one-time experience led to the home birth of a baby on January 29, 1954, with the help of a midwife. It is said that the unsuspecting father, 250 miles away, received a birth announcement along with a hastily scribbled note, "Send clothes." And with that inauspicious beginning, a woman who would bring so much change to our world was born.

Not long after Oprah's birth, her mother left her in the care of grandparents—as so many young mothers have had to do—while she searched for a job and a better life in Wisconsin. Her bleak situation in Mississippi echoed the Great Migrations of years past, when black families left the South to escape the lack of respect, the lack of jobs, and unequal treatment under the law.

## NURTURING OF A QUEEN

*but those who hope in the Lord will renew their strength. They will soar on wings like eagles; they will run and not grow weary, they will walk and not be faint.*
—Isaiah 40:31 (NIV)

The decision by her mother to leave may have been for economic reasons, but it turned out to be a godsend for Oprah. According to most experts, the first five years of a child's life are critical to language and communication development. Although no one could have known it at the time, her grandmother Hattie Mae bestowed those exact gifts upon the young Oprah, helping her build a foundation for the consummate communicator she would one day become.

Oprah lived with her strict grandparents through the age of six in an isolated farmhouse with no indoor plumbing. Hattie Mae, from whom she learned her spiritual values, also taught her to read at an early age (even though, as you will recall, she herself did not write). The church was the center of Hattie Mae's life, and she immersed Oprah in her church community, where Oprah found love and acceptance.

Remarkably, Oprah could recite poems and Bible verses by age three. One Sunday when she was two and a half, she stood in front of her church congregation and touched their hearts when she told them about how "Jesus rose on Easter Day." Feats like this earned her the apt nickname of "the Preacher." Although living on the farm was difficult and her grandmother a strict disciplinarian, Oprah felt loved by her supportive grandmother and church family, who cherished her and recognized her as a very special youngster.

She was so gifted, in fact, that almost as soon as entering kindergarten, Oprah wrote a letter to her teacher explaining why she should advance to the first grade—and it worked. Oprah would also manage to skip second grade. She was always an avid reader, and she jumped at every opportunity to recite poetry in church and clubs, so much so that she earned another title, "the Little Speaker," from the regular crowds who witnessed her performances.

Oprah had few toys growing up. However, she did have a corncob doll. She was a chatterbox and would often lecture her doll and the crows sitting on the fence at the farm. Sometimes, she would even entertain herself by playacting in front of an audience of farm animals. The girl who loved to talk would sometimes go too far. Occasionally, she was put in the corner of the dining room, where Hattie Mae would tell her to "sit there with your mouth shut when company comes to call." Oprah has said that her grandmother often told her that her wish was for Oprah to have a "good white family" to take care of her. She added, "Today, my grandmother, if still alive, would be astonished at the number of good white folks that are working for me."

## ROAD TO RESILIENCY

*Every time you suppress some part of yourself or allow others to play you small, you are in essence ignoring the owner's manual your creator gave you and destroying your design.*
—Oprah Winfrey

Oprah's grandmother Hattie Mae became ill when she was six, and soon Oprah had to leave the security of the farm and her church family—the only life she'd known—to live in an inner-city ghetto of Milwaukee. There, her mother lived in a boarding house, working long hours as a housemaid. Oprah missed the farm and her long talks with the farm animals, so the imaginative girl made pets out of the only animals around, the insects.

Oprah herself knew she was a smart child. "The one element," she says, "the prevailing element in my life that allowed me not to be embittered or feel discriminated against is that I had an education. I never felt less than a white kid. White people never made me feel less. Black people made me feel less." In particular, she recalls Miss Miller, a very light-skinned black lady who owned and ran the boarding house where Oprah lived with her mother and half-sister. Appallingly, Miss Miller would tell Oprah she didn't like her because her skin was too dark and her hair too kinky. Miss Miller would send Oprah out at night to the small porch to sleep. Imagine how awful Oprah must have felt, curled up all alone, not allowed in the house with the rest of her family.

Oprah lived with her mother that time for only a year. She was then shuttled to Tennessee at age seven to live with her father and stepmother. For the first time, she experienced the joy of having her own room with her own bed. One year later, she left the safety of her father's home for a summer visit to her mother.

Even though her father originally planned to retrieve Oprah in the fall, he could see that, for some reason, Oprah wanted to stay in Milwaukee. Maybe it was the natural urge of a child to remain close to her mother. Maybe it was a fantasy of caring for her mother. Whatever made her give up the relative safety and calm life with her father, she stayed. However, her mother stilled worked long hours, which left Oprah alone in the company of the television, spawning her first dreams of fame and fortune.

Oprah's dramatic flair has always kept life interesting for those around her, according to several sources. When she suspected that her mother was about to give away her puppy, she invented a story of her courageous puppy fending off would-be robbers. It worked, but only until her mother saw through the deception. However, she outdid herself when she convinced Aretha Franklin that she was an abandoned child. Franklin said she recalls giving her $100. Oprah reportedly stayed in a hotel until a minister talked her into going home.

These lighter moments are not to overshadow the hellish life Oprah lived. In Milwaukee, Oprah was often left with relatives who treated her as an insignificant thing rather than the extraordinary person she was. Starting when she was only nine years old, two male relatives and a family friend continually molested her, until she ran away at age 13. One of the predators who assaulted her at age nine would take her out afterward for ice cream, apparently to soothe Oprah's emotional state before her mother got home.

The effects of the abuse were what you might expect. Oprah ultimately was sent to juvenile detention for repeatedly running away from home. After being denied admission because the beds were full, the hapless young teen was returned to the place from which she had so desperately tried to escape.

Like most molested children, Oprah felt shame, carrying this nearly unspeakable truth until she was grown. It would not be until 1986—during an episode of her show—that she revealed the painful experiences. It was only then she finally was able to rid herself of the shame and realize that she "was not responsible for the abuse." In overcoming her own shame, Oprah became increasingly aware that she could use her talk show as an avenue through which her guests could also overcome their greatest barriers to joy.

## WHO WILL SAVE THE QUEEN?

*In the same way, let your light shine before others, that they may see*
*your good deeds and glorify your Father in heaven.*
—Matthew 5:16 (NIV)

Determined to escape the abuse and shed the shackles of the inner city, Oprah once again ran away. It was now apparent to her mother that she could not control her (justifiably) rebellious child, and Oprah once again was sent to live with her father. She only desired a better life, and this time, she was happy to move back to Nashville, even though her father was a strict disciplinarian.

Without knowing it, Oprah's father was accepting not only his daughter, but also her unborn child. Shortly after moving back, Oprah learned that she was pregnant, and managed to conceal it for several months. On the day she finally told her father, Oprah—at age 14—went into early labor and gave birth to a son. The baby died in the hospital soon after.

Oprah's father stood by her and made sure she had a secure home, which allowed her to make the most of her life. Every other week, her stepmother took Oprah to the library to pick out five books. Her father required her to read at least one book a week and to write a corresponding book report. He would send Oprah to bed without dinner unless she learned five new words each day. He would not accept anything less than what he thought was her best. And the gifted child again began to flourish.

Oprah attended church regularly with her father and stepmother and started feeling secure and happy once again. She also began making speeches at social events and churches, once earning $500 for a single speech. At that point, she knew that, beyond a doubt, she wanted to become a paid speaker.

## A QUEEN ON FIRE

*What matters is how you choose to love, how you choose to express
that love through your work, through your family, through what
you have to give to the world.*
—Oprah Winfrey

At the impressionable and tender age of 16, Oprah came upon Maya
Angelou's autobiography *I Know Why the Caged Bird Sings*. "I read it over
and over," she recounts. "I had never before read a book that validated my
own existence." A turning point, Oprah began to concentrate even more
on education and public speaking. She would become an exceptional
student and thrive in all of her extracurricular activities from drama to
debate to student council.

Her hard work and natural gifts began being noticed. In 1970,
she won an Elks Club speaking competition; her prize was a four-year
college scholarship. At 17, Oprah was chosen to attend the White
House Conference on Youth in Colorado, representing Tennessee along
with one other student. Upon returning home, she was interviewed by
WVOL radio, and soon after, the station asked her to represent it in
the Miss Fire Prevention beauty pageant. She was the first black woman
to win the contest. The radio station asked her to work part time as a
newsreader, a job she readily accepted.

Soon after, Oprah was crowned Miss Black Tennessee and was
subsequently offered an on-air job at a radio station serving Nashville's
African-American community. Oprah used her full scholarship to attend
Tennessee State University, where she majored in speech communication
and the performing arts. Upon graduation, she signed on with a local
television station as a reporter and anchor. She was Nashville's first
African-American female to co-anchor the evening news. Oprah was on
fire. She was only 19 years old and a sophomore in college.

She undoubtedly had made her father proud.

At 22, Oprah moved to Baltimore, Maryland, to join WJZ-TV as a news co-anchor; it was there she hosted her first television talk show, the local *People Are Talking*, while continuing to serve as anchor and news reporter. She had found her niche, a profession ideally suited to her outgoing personality and heart of gold. She was loved by almost everyone she reached over the airwaves, although epithets, slurs, and other derogatory comments—none worth mentioning—sometimes hurled her way. Nevertheless, the comments only seemed to make Oprah all the more determined to overcome racial bias by increasingly reaching out to the community.

By age 30, her reputation as an empathetic and adored personality began spreading to other cities. Later, she was invited to Chicago to host a poorly rated morning show in hopes of improving its ratings. In less than a year, the dynamic young woman turned the failing show into the hottest act in town. In less than five years, the program was renamed *The Oprah Winfrey Show*.

## NOW SOARING

> *Turn your wounds into wisdom.*
> —Oprah Winfrey

Oprah's career quickly took her to almost unimaginable heights. In less than a year, *The Oprah Winfrey Show* became number one in national syndication. She won Daytime Emmys for Outstanding Host, Outstanding Talk/ Service Program, and Outstanding Direction. The following year, Oprah was the youngest person in history to receive the International Radio and Television Society's Broadcaster of the Year Award.

Being at the top of the broadcast world might be enough for some people, but Oprah added acting to her resume in a big way in the 1985

Steven Spielberg film, *The Color Purple*. Adapted from Alice Walker's novel of the same name, her performance earned Oprah Best Supporting Actress nominations for both the Golden Globe and Academy Awards. Perhaps more significantly, her outstanding performance as Sofia captured the nation's attention and hearts.

Critics hailed her again for her performance in *Native Son*, a movie adaptation of Richard Wright's classic 1940 novel.

By now, Oprah knew she loved acting and knew she wanted to bring quality entertainment to the industry. For this, she decided to form a production company, Harpo Productions, in 1986 to provide films and television shows to the public. Harpo Studios also provided the vehicle for magazine—and, later, Internet—publishing. Oprah acquired the ownership and production responsibilities for *The Oprah Winfrey Show*, making her the first woman in history to own and produce her own talk show. She would go on to produce the made-for-television movies *The Women of Brewster Place* (1989), *There Are No Children Here* (1993), and *Before Women Had Wings* (1997).

In the 1990s, Oprah began emphasizing the spiritual values she first experienced in her early years at her grandparents' house, and her shows became more popular than ever. She used her memories of childhood abuse to spearhead a campaign for the establishment of a database of convicted child abusers and predators, available to law enforcement agencies across the country. It helped raise parental awareness and gave victims voices. Oprah was already a burgeoning influence in the publishing industry, and her reach and inspiration mushroomed when she began an on-air book club in 1996. Her selections would become instant bestsellers; she herself went on to author numerous books.

No matter her success, Oprah continues to embrace the special friends she has made over her lifetime. Her best friend (since their 20s) is still Gayle King; Oprah has declared, "There isn't a definition in our culture for this kind of bond between women." She also has a longtime friendship with Maria Shriver, which began after they met in Baltimore many years ago. Oprah considers the late Maya Angelou a mentor and friend, calling Maya her "mother-sister-friend." Since 1986, Oprah has called Stedman Graham her partner. He and Oprah became engaged in 1996, although they never married.

In late 2010, the woman who loves to surprise others came into a remarkable discovery of her own: she had a half-sister she had known nothing about for 47 years. She introduced her viewers to Patricia Lee in 2011, tearfully sharing that Patricia had found out about their link three years earlier and was a woman of such great character that, despite initial rebuffs from their mother, she had chosen not to sell their story or take it to the press.

Oprah—who also gained a niece and nephew from the discovery—bought Patricia a beautiful home in Wisconsin in early 2014 and will ensure that her sister's dream of attending college will become a reality.

May 25, 2011, was the final broadcast of *The Oprah Winfrey Show*. Shortly after that, Oprah began hosting the primetime show *Oprah's Lifeclass*, from October 2011 until September 2014, on OWN, the Oprah Winfrey Network. OWN itself debuted on January 1, 2011, in approximately 80 million homes. Heralded as "more than a television network, it's a network of people just like YOU," Harpo Productions and Discovery Communications produce the general entertainment television channel.

Oprah is the highest-paid performer on television and the richest woman in America. More significantly, her profound influence is immeasurable, with her name appearing on every world list of leading opinion makers. "Arguably the most influential woman in the world" (as stated by *The American Spectator*). Oprah, among other recognitions, has been in the Time 100—*Time* magazine's annual list of the 100 most influential people in the world—nine times (each year from 2004 through 2011, plus for the twentieth century), a feat rivaled only by

President Barack Obama. Oprah's accomplishments and involvements are so vast that it's difficult to list all her business and other interests, which extend well beyond her own production company.

It's interesting to note that, in *Finding Oprah's Roots*, Oprah is quoted as saying, "Before I have a big meeting or decision to make, I go, and I sit with the ancestors. Literally, I go and sit in my closet, and I say their names. I just say their names so that when I walk into the space, I don't walk alone."

## OPRAH'S THOUGHTS

### On Success
"Think like a queen. A queen is not afraid to fail. Failure is another steppingstone to greatness."

### On Education and Reading
"For me, education is about the most important thing because that is what liberated me. The ability to read saved my life. I would have been an entirely different person had I not been taught to read at an early age. My entire life experience, my ability to believe in myself, and even in my darkest moments of sexual and physical abuse and so forth, I knew there was another way. I knew there was a way out. I knew there was another kind of life because I had read about it. I knew there were other places, and there was another way of being. It saved my life, so that's why I now focus my attention on trying to do the same thing for other people."

### On Money
"What I know is, if you do what you love, and the work fulfills you, the rest will come. I truly believe that the reason I've been able to be so financially successful is because my focus has never, ever for one minute,

been on the money. And the fact that money has come has surprised me. But the money has never been the focus. You know you are on the road to success if you would do your job and not be paid for it. It's like being able to say, 'I would do this job and take on a second job to make ends meet, even if nobody paid me— just for the opportunity to do it!' If you can say that, that's how you know you are doing the right thing."

## On the Key to a Fulfilling Life

"I think the most important thing to get ahead falls back to what I truly believe in, and that is the ability to seek truth in your life. That's all forms. You have to be honest with yourself. You can't be pursuing a profession because your parents say it's the best thing, because you think you will make a lot of money, or because you think you are going to get attention. None of that will do you any good if you are not honest with yourself."

## OPRAH'S SUCCESS TIPS

- "The big secret in life is that there is no big secret. Whatever your goal, you can get there if you're willing to work.
- Energy is the essence of life. Every day, you decide how you're going to use it by knowing what you want and what it takes to reach that goal and by maintaining focus.
- For every one of us who succeeds, it's because there's somebody there to show you the way out. The light doesn't always necessarily have to be in your family; for me, it was teachers and school.
- I don't believe in failure. It is not failure if you enjoyed the process.
- I don't think of myself as a poor, deprived ghetto girl who made good. I think of myself as somebody who from an early age knew I was responsible for myself, and I had to make good.

- I feel that luck is preparation meeting opportunity.
- What material success does is provide you with the ability to concentrate on other things that really matter. And that is being able to make a difference, not only in your own life but in other people's lives.
- You *can* have it all. You just can't have it all at once.
- You know you are on the road to success if you would do your job and not be paid for it.
- The key to realizing a dream is to focus not on success but significance—and then even the small steps and little victories along your path will take on greater meaning."

These beliefs reveal a woman on a mission to reach her full, God-given potential. Oprah is a Queen of Queens, flying to heights most of us only dream of reaching. How could she have known that one day she would become America's beloved best friend, seen and heard by millions? And could she have known that she would become the first African-American female billionaire, considered far and wide to be one of the world's most generous people, helping many generations to come? Oprah's shining example paves the way for others to realize their own potentials and possibilities, if only they, too, believe they can fly.

### Write Your Goals for Success

_____

_____

_____

_____

_____

_____

(Go to www.GodGaveUsWings.com for a free worksheet.)

## PAY IT FORWARD

*I've come to believe that each of us has a personal calling that's as unique as a fingerprint—and that the best way to succeed is to discover what you love and then find a way to offer it to others in the form of service, working hard, and also allowing the energy of the universe to lead you.*

—Oprah Winfrey

After Oprah's role in establishing the database for law enforcement and its far-reaching impact on the lives of countless children, she clearly saw how well-directed funding and endorsements could make big, important changes.

Even as she built her financial empire, making her the first African-American female billionaire, her generosity grew. She continued to pour out to others in need, making her one of the world's most generous philanthropists. In 2000, Oprah's Angel Network began presenting $100,000 Use Your Life Award to people who have committed their lives to helping others. Over the years, she has spearheaded numerous philanthropic programs, which include a school near Johannesburg, South Africa, the Oprah Winfrey Leadership Academy for Girls. Oprah's legendary generosity extends to her beloved viewers. In her celebrated show's 2004 season, she created a massive "joy rising" moment on national television when she gave every person in the studio audience a new car. In 2011, the Academy of Motion Picture Arts and Sciences recognized her philanthropy with a special Oscar statuette, the Jean Hersholt Humanitarian Award. In 2013, President Barack Obama awarded Oprah with the nation's highest civilian honor, the Presidential Medal of Freedom.

In spite of her very active schedule, Oprah frequently takes the time to give free lectures at churches, shelters, and youth organizations.

To top it off, she hosts a weekly self-help talk show, *Super Soul Sunday*, in which she discusses spirituality, the meaning of life, and her belief in God.

Oprah's first desires to learn—born from a long line of family members who put education first—have expanded, blossomed, and subsequently rippled outward to affect positively many viewers, listeners, and readers over the decades.

### List a Few Ways You Can Help Others

_____

_____

_____

_____

_____

## BLESSING PRAYER

My prayer for you is that God will bless you with huge dreams, keeping you in His arms until you are strong enough to fly on your own. And when you are ready, may He throw you so high in the air that you soar greater than ever imagined! May God bless you on your journey and keep you safe during your life's travels. Amen.

## NEXT CHAPTER

This heartfelt story is about a young Laotian girl's journey with her brave mother who was determined to find her beloved husband. He was a freedom fighter, captured and imprisoned by North Vietnamese Communist soldiers. Little did this family know that their journey would take them over 10,000 miles to their Promised Land.

## CHAPTER 2

# An Immigrant's Journey

*For I know the plans I have for you," declares the Lord, "plans to prosper you and not to harm you, plans to give you hope and a future. Then you will call on me and come and pray to me, and I will listen to you. You will seek me and find me when you seek me with all your heart.*

Jeremiah 29:11-13 (NIV)

### JOURNEY OF HOPE

I t was 1973 in Laos, a country left in tatters after the Vietnam War. The girl in this story, Keo, was born into a Buddhist family. When she was but two years old, before forming a bond she could remember, her father, a freedom fighter, was captured and imprisoned by Communist soldiers. During her father's imprisonment, Keo lived with her mother's parents, an experience that shaped fond childhood memories. One extraordinarily warm memory is of the excitement she felt when her grandfather let her ride a water buffalo around the farm.

Six years later, news came to Seng, Keo's mother, that her husband had survived prison and was likely living in a Thailand refugee camp. Although only a rumor, the next thing the child knew, she and her younger sister were packing to go to Thailand—no questions asked, no information given, only that they were leaving the very same night. Upon reaching the Mekong River crossing, the small family beheld an excessive number of enemy patrol boats. The risks were too great. Seng turned her daughters around and took them back to her parents' home, where they were welcomed once again with open arms. The unsuccessful trip did not deter the girls' mother from a subsequent attempt to find her beloved husband of eight years. This time, Seng asked her father to guide them on the dangerous journey that would again take them on foot for three days and three nights to reach the Mekong River and cross over to Thailand.

The brave man agreed to take his cherished family as far as he could and then hired two fishermen to take them the rest of the way, across the river and onward. Soon after saying their goodbyes, Seng saw soldiers approaching with guns. She grabbed her daughters and immediately jumped into the bushes to hide. Some time later, the fishermen motioned that the soldiers were gone, and it was safe to get into the boat. As they approached the water, the horrified eight-year-old witnessed at least 10 corpses floating facedown in the river—the bodies of families killed while trying to cross over. Little did the girl know that she was just one of two million Vietnamese who attempted to escape to Thailand, Malaysia, and the Philippines over the 10-year period from 1975 to 1985. Seeking passages to freedom, as many as half a million people drowned during this tragic mass exodus.

## CALL UPON ME, AND I WILL LISTEN

*So do not fear, for I am with you; do not be dismayed, for I am your*
*God. I will strengthen you and help you; I will uphold you with my*
*righteous right hand.*
—Isaiah 41:10 (NIV)

It was now late, and the weather began to turn for the worse. The
fishermen feared that if they didn't act quickly, they would not get their
human cargo across the river in time. As the two girls lay flat in the
bottom of the smelly fishing boat, Seng covered their small bodies with
her own to protect them from potential gunfire. They all knew their
lives depended upon complete invisibility. As she cradled them, Seng
whispered, "Don't say a word; if you do, you will get us killed!"

Rowing quietly, the two fishermen knew that the darkness most
likely obscured the view of the Laotian soldiers, who had strict orders to
execute anyone trying to escape the war-torn country. Suddenly, there
was a storm. The high winds rocked the boat. The rain soaked their
bodies, but thankfully, the thunder masked their screams.

The next thing Keo remembers was her devout Buddhist mother
crying out to God, the One "she nonetheless knew," "Prajow soy dae!
God help us!" She recalls, "Almost immediately, the storm subsided, and
a great calm came over the water. I believe that even though we didn't
believe in God, He believed in us, covering the eyes and ears of the
soldiers! It had to be God; how else would we have landed safely on the
other side?" A loaded hay wagon moved toward them, and the family
quickly jumped in and hid under the mounds of hay; they were not to
come out until told. Their fate lay in the hands of strangers who had
been paid to smuggle them into Thailand.

Keo's family made it safely to Thailand. Once transported to a
refugee camp, they would live there for the next year. The cramped

sleeping quarters were a snug fit for three people; restroom functions were carried out in the fields, for everyone to see. Rations were meager, and the girls knew that if they were to survive, they all had to work. Keo and her sister, who was only six years old, found jobs carrying fresh water for a landowner in exchange for their daily food, with their mother working as a cook. "Even though we did not call on God or know who He was," Keo affirms today, "He continued to do miracles and bring people to our path."

To their astonishment, Keo's mother discovered that the landowner for whom they'd been carrying water for was, in fact, her husband's best friend. The landowner shared that their father, Paul, had lived in the same camp but had recently immigrated to America. The owner contacted Paul, putting in motion events that would someday lead to the reuniting of Keo's family.

## THE PROMISED LAND

> ... nor is a messenger greater than the one who sent him. Now that you know these things, you will be blessed if you do them.
> —John 13:16-17 (NIV)

One year and three refugee camps later, the family readied themselves to leave Thailand for the United States. The First Baptist Church in Amarillo, Texas, a city designated as a resettlement zone for Vietnamese refugees, also agreed to help the small Laotian family. Finally approved for immigration to America and leaving behind the fear of death, the family boarded an airplane for the first time in their lives, flying nearly 10,000 miles and 36 hours to reach their final destination. Seng and the girls, especially Keo, were filled with excitement. Imagine what must have been going through Keo's head—she was traveling to a place she thought of as the Promised Land to meet her father, in the company of a mother who had risked their lives to find him.

Their plane finally touched down in Amarillo, where Keo's father nervously awaited. Although Keo was excited to meet her dad, she recalls, "I finally met my father face-to-face in 1981. Even though it was a great reunion, I had a lot of bitterness and anger because I didn't understand why my father left and never explained why. But God started to change that quickly."

After eight long years, Keo's family was finally reunited. Her mother was overjoyed to have her treasured husband back after the Communists had taken him from her those many years ago. Keo wasn't feeling so warm and fuzzy toward her father, however. Rather, she was feeling a little jealous, because now she had to share her mother with someone she barely knew. Admittedly, it took some time before Keo felt like they were all one family.

The local church aiding Keo's family stepped in upon their arrival, assigning mentors for each family member to acquaint them with the American way. Keo and Kack, her younger sister, were enrolled in school. Keo went into the second grade, where her father made her stay for three years until she learned English. Keo reports that she had the same teacher that entire time, a woman who luckily possessed lots of patience and love for Keo throughout those years. How overwhelming it must have been for this family who spoke no English, in a foreign country, with limited education, and living in a city with over 186,300 people, especially when compared to their tiny village in Laos!

Keo's mother and grandmother always told her she was a sickly child because she would get sick after consuming her meals of fish and rice (through the grace of God, doctors finally discovered she was allergic to fish when Keo was a teenager). Perhaps this was the dubious reason behind when Keo's grandfather paid them a visit from Laos in 1986, he bore the "gift" of a cassette tape on which Keo's grandmother proclaimed that (among other things) she would always love Keo, even though she was not pretty. Most 13-year-old girls would be at least troubled, if not damaged, by such a remark, but not Keo: since, "she could do little about her outer appearance, she would do everything possible to become beautiful on the inside."

## SEEK ME AND FIND ME

> *"... as for me and my household, we will serve the Lord."*
> —Joshua 24:15 (NIV)

First Baptist Church became Keo's second family, especially her mentors, Delbert and Mary Lou Serratt and Mrs. Pat Chamberlain, all of whom guided her throughout her life: "God protected us and gave us many earth angels who would help us along our journey." Keo recalls that her family still practiced Buddhism, even though the girls and their mother (but not their father) attended church. Keo's father finally agreed to go once—on Father's Day Sunday—to appease his family. The sermon told how "God gave His only begotten Son" to save us. The next thing Keo remembers: "It took only one encounter with God to change my dad from a man who was bitter to a man full of joy and peace. It was a life-changing experience for our family when Dad, on his knees, asked Jesus to be his Lord and Savior."

When they got home from church that day, Keo's father, in turn, asked her mother, "Seng, will you choose Christ or Buddha?" It was not an easy decision to make: among other things, how would Keo's illiterate mother even learn the teachings of her husband's newfound religion? But Seng hesitated only briefly before her answer sprang forth: "I will follow Christ." It would take over five years for Keo's father, working with his wife every night, to teach her to read from the Bible.

According to Keo, "My father changed after being saved that Father's Day Sunday. He was no longer a bitter or angry man. Instead, he was more joyful and became a more patient and loving father. I was particularly grateful because there were no more spankings!" Shortly after that, her father gained a sense of purpose and became an ordained minister. And Keo knew she wanted that same sense of purpose and joy, just like her father. She was baptized four months later, at the age of 12. Keo began the next segment of her life's journey.

## LIFE CHALLENGE

*Don't let anyone look down on you because you are young, but set an example for the believers in speech, in conduct, in love, in faith and in purity.*
—1 Timothy 4:12 (NIV)

Keo was a teenager now. Her father began worrying about his daughter and wondering how he was going to protect her from the crime, gangs, and drugs—as well as teen pregnancies—running rampant in the Laotian-American community. Paul, a godly man, gave his daughter a life challenge while she was still in the eighth grade; he told Keo that if she saved herself for marriage, he would both pay for her college and buy her a new car. Keo jumped at the challenge. Since she was, at the time, more interested in the thought of a car rather than of a boyfriend.

While talking to her mentor Mary Lou Serratt, Keo shared her father's life challenge with her. Mary Lou encouraged Keo to write out a prayer that detailed her prerequisites for a husband. The top two were "has to be tall and handsome" and "has to treat me like a queen." Keo took her father's challenge to heart and focused on giving of herself by helping others transition into their new American lives.

After graduating from college, Keo agreed to attend nursing school to honor her parents' wishes. As a sophomore there, she met her future husband, Henry Chan, while on a mission trip to Birmingham, Alabama. Upon meeting Henry for the first time, her immediate reaction was that he was too short to be her future husband. Later, to Keo's great surprise, she discovered this was the same guy Mary Lou Serratt had met one month earlier in Fort Worth, Texas: Mary Lou had sent her a picture of Henry, exclaiming, "This is your future husband!"

Henry didn't look anything like the man in Keo's dreams and prayers, and Keo was initially frightened by the thought of such a life-changing decision. However, after asking for confirmation from God (and receiving it through her sister, Kack), she knew she wanted to spend her life with Henry "because of his love of Christ and his heart for the lost." Keo also learned that she and Henry had been in the same Thailand refugee camp at the same time; they had even simultaneously immigrated to America. Their fathers were both freedom fighters; Keo and Henry both felt they were called to full-time missions in high school, and each had prayed that their future spouse would remain pure.

After the mission trip, Keo returned, unavoidably, to Amarillo, and Henry went back to Fort Worth, where he was a youth pastor. Over the next two and a half years, they would correspond, discovering more and more of each other's wonderful qualities, until Henry asked Keo if he could court her until marriage. Keo now fully realized what a giant of a man Henry was and that he more than surpassed her dreams for a husband! Another year and a half later, after Keo's graduation from nursing school in 1998, Keo's lifelong mentor Dr. Delbert Serratt married the two.

Regretfully, the couple's dreams of a family were soon crushed by the loss of not one but two babies to miscarriage. Keo recalls that she "never got angry but did begin questioning God if we would ever have children." Prayerfully, Keo and Henry relinquished control of their family to God. Not long after that, they were blessed with a boy, Kaleb, and six years later with a baby girl, Caroline.

## LIFE'S VOCATION

After the children had been born, Keo decided to quit working as a nurse to devote her time to being a full-time mother and pastor's wife. The Chan family would take a circular path to end up where they are today—from Euless, Texas, to High Point, North Carolina—all the while busy performing God's work in numerous ways. As Keo puts it, "We were not focusing on full-time missions. We were half obedient, which is full disobedience." Henry enrolled in seminary, where, as Keo says, "God taught me to bloom where I am." After Henry's graduation from seminary, Keo continues, "Our hearts just wanted to go back home to Laos and Thailand and share the gospel with our people." Unfortunately, those dreams were not realized, because of the International Mission Board regulations surrounding medical issues. Keo recalls, "God was silent for three months, and then He said, 'I'm giving you the same heartbeat, the same vision, the same people, just not in Thailand.'"

Today, Henry is associate pastor of discipleship and family ministries at Northwest Baptist Church in Oklahoma City, the metropolis where he has also worked to establish a second-generation Asian church through All Nations Church. Keo works as a residential real estate agent, which gives her the flexibility to work around her schedule as pastor's wife. A devoted Christian in every sense of the word, Keo exemplifies a woman who has not only beaten the odds to achieve success, but also consistently shares that success and joy with others in all realms of her life.

*Peace I leave with you; my peace I give you. I do not give to you as the world gives. Do not let your hearts be troubled and do not be afraid.*

—John 14:27 (NIV)

## KEO'S THOUGHTS ON SUCCESS

- The greatest job is to give back.
- Glorify God's name.
- Give purpose to someone who is lost.
- Show love to someone without love.
- Guide lost souls toward God.
- Help someone back after they have helped you.
- Give joyfully.
- Give time.
- Teach others how to pray.
- Pray blessings over others.

Like the other women in this book, Keo did not stop after a few years of service. Instead, she continues to use her life lessons to help others succeed. Her journey has been tough, but it has also taught her resilience, trust, honor, discipline, faith, and—above all—to believe in God. Take action today…it's never too late to soar!

### Write Your Goals for Success

_____

_____

_____

_____

_____

(Go to www.GodGaveUsWings.com for a free worksheet.)

## PAY IT FORWARD

*Give, and it will be given to you. A good measure, pressed down,*
*shaken together and running over, will be poured into your lap. For*
*with the measure you use, it will be measured to you.*
—Luke 6:38 (NIV)

Keo first gave back to her community when she was only a teen, spending countless hours acting as a translator for newly arriving Laotian refugees. Once thought of by some as an ugly duckling, she has blossomed into a beautiful woman from the inside out.

Keo says, "God has planted in me the same heart and the same desire to train up and mentor other women. To have the heart for my community to think locally and globally…I pray that Henry and I will be privileged enough to possess even a little bit of what Dr. and Mrs. Serratt modeled throughout their lives."

As Keo strives to be more like her mentors, she continues to look for ways to give back to her community and is part of the organization Women of the World, which sponsors 50 women at a time from various countries. The women live in the community, where they are given guidance throughout their transition into the American way of life—for instance, learning how to cook, dress, drive a car, or even go to the movies, things that many of us sometimes take for granted. Keo remembers one young woman in particular. She was about 20 years old and already a mother of two small children, who was pregnant with an unexpected third child and was contemplating either suicide or abortion. Keo prayed with her for hours for God to guide her and protect her in His loving arms. She stayed with the girl until she decided to accept life over death for both herself and the child, and took God into her life.

## VOLUNTEERING AND AWARDS

Through the years, Keo has ministered to others in a multitude of ways. She has volunteered in locations from nursing homes to Woman's Missionary Union (WMU) retreats. She has been a part of backyard Bible clubs—often leading Bible studies—and a WMU Girls in Action summer camp counselor and international Sunday school teacher.

In 1993, Keo was named a National Acteens Panelist by National WMU, and now sponsors other young ladies. Each year, the WMU names only six high school seniors as National Acteens Panelists for their commitment to missions and their participation and leadership in their Acteens group, church, school, and community. Acteens is a missions organization for girls in grades 7–12 sponsored by WMU, in which girls grow in their relationship with God and each other as they participate in missions and develop leadership skills.

### List a Few Ways You Can Help Others

_____
_____
_____
_____
_____

## BLESSING PRAYER

May God bless you with peace and with the courage to follow God's prompting, by removing any fears of flying toward an amazing life, and as you soar, may you fall in love with the sky given to you through His grace! Amen.

## NEXT CHAPTER

The next chapter is about a woman who has a smile as big as Dallas and who, over the years, saw her life take drastic turns—from the good, to the bad, to the ugly, and back again full circle. Her story recounts the triumphant of overcoming her darkest hours: her father's betrayal of his young family, feelings of abandonment by her mother, ongoing verbal and emotional abuse at the hands of the man she loved, and the extraordinary health challenges she endured.

CHAPTER 3

# Life, Full Circle

*Do not conform to the pattern of this world, but be transformed by the renewing of your mind. Then you will be able to test and approve what God's will is...*
—Romans 12:2 (NIV)

## A WINDING ROAD

This is a story about a woman who has a smile as big as Dallas and who was born in Fort Worth, Texas, a town with 150 years of Western heritage, "where the West begins." Her Texas roots, which doubtlessly helped form her big Texas personality, have always played an important part in her life.

Over the years, Sue saw her life take drastic turns—from the good, to the bad, to the ugly, and back again full circle. Her story recounts the triumphant of overcoming her darkest hours: her father's betrayal of his young family, feelings of abandonment by her mother, ongoing verbal and emotional abuse at the hands of the man she loved, and the extraordinary health challenges she endured.

Over time, Sue would realize the adverse effects that her parents' and husband's demeanors had on her self-esteem. To offset the negativity, she invented positive aphorisms to motivate herself and to neutralize the impact of others and her destructive self-talk. Today, this professional speaker, success coach, and author shares her techniques for achieving a happier life around the world.

## FIRST IMPRESSIONS

The first of five children, Sue was born to two hardworking people in the grocery business. Shortly after Sue's birth, her mother became a stay-at-home mom. Happy days seemed there to stay, extending through the births of the other four babies. Although, we all know first impressions can be deceiving, just like most TV shows are fiction. In the early years, this family was a perfect portrayal of the 1950s—described mostly as an affectionate, loving, and loyal family—then one day, it all came tumbling down.

Sue started out as one of those lucky kids, an adored child especially cherished by her grandparents. However, there were many challenges in this family—to start with, for the first three years, their firstborn child was covered from head to toe with a horrible rash. The family's physician diagnosed baby Sue with asthma and severe eczema, which later subsided to only the bends of her arms and the backs of her legs. Doctors determined she was allergic to milk, eggs, wheat, chocolate, and much more. Needless to say, Sue felt deprived of the "good stuff" that all of the other kids her age got to eat. Finally, Sue's parents accepted, out of sheer desperation and years of ineffective treatments, that, no matter what, their child would suffer from eczema. Now, imagine the joy of this child hearing for the first time that she could eat all the junk food she wanted, just like her friends.

Sue loved visiting her mother's parents, who lived near the rodeo grounds—especially when her grandfather took her to look for money under the bleachers. He taught her a valuable lesson: "You can always find money if you just look for it." Little Sue was now about to start school, and her mother wanted to expand on her grandfather's lesson by teaching her the value of money. Sue recalls, "Mother paid me a 25-cent weekly allowance for doing chores. My mother would then charge me 5 cents each day for the bologna sandwich for my school lunch." This child quickly learned the value of a nickel.

Some of Sue's fondest memories include visits to her father's parents on the weekends. They lived in the small Texas town of Clairette. The young girl had big dreams of singing solo on stage—maybe, one day, in front of her grandparents' church congregation. Her adoring grandmother told her, "Sue, I love you way too much to allow you to embarrass yourself and me at church; instead, you can read a Bible verse." So, on Sundays after church, Sue read the longest passage she could find, until her little sister would cry out, "Please, make her stop!" These readings eventually led to a talent show in the third grade (complete with big, puffy poodle skirt). Sue was, for the first time, living her dream, singing and dancing her little heart out in front of a live audience. All the while, her proud father watched from the back.

Sue loved to perform and to write stories. This creative fourth-grader wrote a play, *The Queen of Hearts*, in which, after recruiting others to be in the play, she held the starring role as the queen. The talented girl sold tickets to all the little actors' and actresses' parents and donated the money to the Milk and Ice Fund, a charity that provided "needy mothers and their infants" with milk and with ice for storing perishables. The Fort Worth newspaper picked up the story, and Sue was thrilled with the publicity. This powerful life lesson taught Sue a multitude of skills —recruitment, sales, negotiation, and how to effectively channel her creativity—all things she would use later in life.

## SPIRALING DOWNHILL

However, Sue's life began to spiral downhill. Sue said, "Mother could no longer tolerate dad's years of infidelity and decided it was time to become financially self-sufficient if she had to support her children." Sue was in the fifth grade when her mother left to live with her brother and attend his beauty school in Wichita Falls. She took the younger two children with her, leaving Sue and two other siblings behind with her father. Sue says as an adult, "I didn't remember being all that upset— until Dad told me that I cried myself to sleep every night until Mother returned two years later." This was about the time Sue began the seventh grade. Imagine how excited she felt to have her mother finally home. I am sure Sue's mom thought that her absence made her husband's heart grow fonder– but that was not the case.

Two years can be a lifetime for some, but apparently not so much for Sue's dad. This man had no desire to have a monogamous marriage but did agree to live together once again as a family. However, he would continue going out with other women. As you might imagine, this drove Sue's mother almost crazy. She would drive around town with her five children in tow, trying to catch him with his mistress. Less than a year later, the marriage ended, shattering Sue's life. Like most children, she was devastated by her parents' divorce, and she vowed at age 12 that she would never get a divorce and inflict this type of pain on her children.

Sue was a ninth grader when her mother decided to remarry…but to whom? Her mother had three potential suitors. So, what else would a mother do except to give her five children the option of choosing their next stepfather? They all gathered 'round on the front porch to discuss the pros and cons of each fellow. If she married one man, they would have to move to Alaska; another man, they would have to deal with his heavy drinking; and last but not least, there was the engineer—and if their mother married him, they could stay in the same schools. The engineer it was, and shortly afterward, her mother and the engineer were married.

Little did Sue know that her new stepfather's employer would transfer him to Mississippi, making her biggest fear a reality, uprooting her from the home she loved and, worse, taking her away from her beloved grandparents. Sue vividly remembers her pronouncement of dislike for Mississippi to all her new schoolmates, declaring, "It is not at all like Texas!" Needless to say, when it was time to move back to Texas, everyone from Mississippi waved goodbye.

Once again, the family moved. This time, to Galveston—it was not Fort Worth, but at least it was Texas. This time, Sue decided to change her mindset and began repeating to herself, "I'm going to love this town, this school, and these people." Not surprisingly, she did love school, and she did make friends quickly. She tried out for the drill team and was successful. She grew where she was planted, and began believing that all things are possible if you believe. This was also the same time that chocolate was introduced into her life as a comfort food. After her mother had read an article that chocolate could give you a surge of energy, her mother began giving Sue a bar every day before drill practice, believing it was helping her child. So, naturally, in her late 20s, when Sue received accolades for outstanding performances on the job, she immediately headed to the local corner store to reward herself with a chocolate bar. It was not until many years later, through therapy, that Sue learned that she ate chocolate when she felt inferior because it made her feel comfortable and loved. Sue discovered the most harmful things we do to ourselves are sometimes connected to our childhood experiences. We all have to learn from our life experiences and learn to control unwanted behaviors. The lesson learned is that if you become aware of challenges and admit to them, then you can work on change.

## THE GREATEST IS LOVE

*And now these three remain: faith, hope and love. But the greatest of these is love.*
— I Corinthians 13:13 (NIV)

At 17, Sue was a new teenage bride, filled with love and anticipation for the future. Shortly after their marriage, her husband went to work at a local grocery store chain, and Sue went to work for a loan company. She recalls the manager's interview questions:

"Do you type?"

"No."

"Do you know shorthand?"

"No."

"Do you have any accounting experience?"

"No."

"Then, what did you take in school?"

"Drama! I was going to be either an actress or a high school drama teacher."

To Sue's complete surprise, the manager hired her, all because of her "big Texas smile." He said people walking past the glass storefront would see her and be drawn inside. At the age of 17, Sue was already executing loans and performing collections while her boss did all the secretarial work. Well, his idea worked: their Location became the company's number one in the state of Texas. See what a simple smile can do!

Things soon changed. Her boss left the company, and Sue didn't connect with the new person; she felt he lacked the drive of her old boss. No matter. Sue and her husband felt they had hit the jackpot when they bought their first brand new brick house with a mere $500 down payment. Shortly afterward, Sue was carrying her first child, who arrived when Sue was only 18. Life was good for this family.

Two years later, Sue's husband lost his job and was replaced by the owner's son. What was this young and now-frightened family of three to do for a mortgage payment? Their only thought was to sell to the first person willing to take over the payments. They later learned that the house had appreciated over those two years and was worth substantially more than their selling price. (The lesson learned here is always to get professional advice before making a major decision.)

Sue's family moved to Dallas, where her husband found a job with a national grocery store chain and Sue with a credit department. This time, she was hired as a secretary, making $240 a month. Helping with collections, she thrived—so much so that her boss wanted her to only do collections and with more pay. However, Sue thought this meant that her boss didn't think she was capable of doing both tasks, so she quit her job. Later, she realized that her boss actually recognized her talents, but because of her low self-esteem, she had sabotaged her own success.

Once again, Sue's life was changing. Her mother and family moved to Greece when her stepfather was transferred. Once again, Sue felt the anguish of abandonment from her childhood. She began eating to try to fill the emptiness of not having her mother nearby.

At age 20, Sue had two children and had gained over 100 pounds from her two pregnancies, the stress, and, most importantly, from suppressing her feelings with emotional eating. To make matters worse, this was an era of thinner women, capturing the Twiggy supermodel look. This period began to have a widespread impact on women's health and self-image—when singer Karen Carpenter was known to have dieted at starvation levels for over a decade, a practice that would later claim her life in 1983.

Many years later, Sue learned that a good relationship depended on mutual communication, if it was to thrive and grow, which was severely lacking in her marriage. The more Sue suppressed her feelings, the more weight she gained—leading to even greater turmoil in her relationship.

Sadly, Sue's husband was clueless about her unhappiness, and since this was a time of extreme thinness, her large-silhouette body became the target of his verbal insults over her weight gain. Sue's self-esteem sunk even lower when her husband said he was ashamed to be seen in public with her. Even today, mass media conditions us to believe that thin is beautiful. What happened to the saying "pretty is as pretty does"?

And what did Sue do when she felt she wasn't good enough? As usual, she outperformed. To help supplement her husband's income, she began selling jewelry in her community. Soon after, Sue was named the jewelry company's top regional recruiter. At its annual banquet, after only three months, the jewelry distributor awarded Sue the distinction of Top Recruiter in the state of Texas. Since her husband felt her job was taking too much time from their children, he asked her to quit the job, and Sue left the place that made her feel worthy. Sue felt disheartened over losing something that made her feel valuable.

*For the Spirit God gave us does not make us timid, but gives us*
*power, love and self-discipline.*
            — 2 Timothy 1:7 (NIV)

Two years later, the family's third child was born, a son that would be named after his father. Sue's husband's company transferred him to Pasadena, Texas, and the family moved to Houston to be near his work. In 1972, their fourth child, a girl, came into the world. Sue tried again to supplement their income, this time by selling Tupperware. In a single week, she sold $1,000 of the product, winning herself two Marlboro coats, one for her and one for her husband. However, again, her husband requested she quit the job; again, he felt it took too much time away from home.

As expected, Sue left her beloved job, but it didn't help their troubled marriage. On Christmas Eve of 1974, her husband announced he was leaving her and the children. "What am I going to do?" Sue anguished. "I have no education, no training, and I am overweight. No one will ever hire me." Her self-esteem and self-confidence plummeted to an all-time low.

And then, Sue's life took a turn.

Her husband didn't leave, after all. Instead, Sue decided to position herself, like her mother, just in case he changed his mind. First, she had to find a job that made her self-reliant, but she had no idea what this job would look like. She did remember her beloved grandmother telling her, "Do what you love, and you will not have to worry about money."

Sue knew she loved to sell, loved people, and loved houses. Now, put all three together, and you've got a top-notch real estate agent. She enrolled at San Jacinto College to get her real estate license, and once she had completed all the courses, the next step was to find someone to hire her. Now, listen carefully to Sue's sabotaging self-talk: *Can I even find a broker? After all, I have no education other than high school, I'm overweight, I have absolutely no experience, and I've got four small children below the age of eight.*

## TAKE ACTION NOW

*The condition you're in at this moment is the product of your previous thoughts, to change your condition, change your thoughts.*
—Debasish Mridha

As might have been expected, Sue, now 27, got a job immediately and was ready to take flight. She shadow the firm's top sales agent, learning as much as possible from this successful woman. She wrote notecards on the step-by-step process of selling houses, which included memorizing the various purchase agreements—except for a cash sale. One time, a couple wanted to pay cash for a house. Sue didn't even think it was possible to buy a house using cash; after all, in her mind, no one had that kind of money. However, Sue needed to buy time to figure out how to write up a cash sale. She told the potential buyers to go home and think about it until the next day. Sue called them the following morning. However, they had changed their minds. (Another valuable lesson learned: Don't put off until tomorrow what you can do today!)

Not surprisingly, Sue sold five houses in her first week as a new agent. Her broker told her, "You are so good at sales that you probably won't be good at getting listings." Sure enough, Sue listed only two houses that first year; all the rest were sales. This trend did not change until the firm hired another agent, one who told Sue that listing really meant the same thing as sales. That's all Sue needed to hear. She sequentially became a listing and selling agent, realizing that selling is actually helping people get what they want while getting what you want, too.

After just one year with the real estate firm, Sue became the top producer in the office, and by the second year, she was declared the top regional producer. Two years later, Sue opened her own real estate company with three partners.

Still suffering from low self-esteem, Sue decided to attend a motivational seminar by Zig Ziglar, where she heard for the first time about goal setting. When Sue saw those speakers on stage, she got a rush, knowing this was her destiny. Sue loved to help people feel good about themselves right now, today, regardless of their situation in life.

Just 29 years old, Sue set a goal of becoming a professional speaker by the time she was 35. That day, she had heard Cavett Robert, a leading motivational speaker, declare, "You can't heat yourself up with snowballs." Once again, Sue thought, *How can I accomplish my goal of becoming a speaker when I have no formal education?* She decided to educate herself by reading one book a week for the next eight years. But, after two years, she realized she didn't remember much of what she had read. She said, "I became more focused on the goal, not the outcome." She began to read the same books over again to make sure she was retaining every nugget of useful information.

Sue refined her process. To better retain the information, she paid her children to log her notes from each book into the computer, further transforming the words into tapes that she could listen to while driving. What Sue didn't realize at first was that her children were also receiving the positive messages from the motivational tapes. During her five-hour drive to visit her parents and beloved grandmother, Sue would listen to motivational and sales technique tapes. Once again, little did she realize that her children were listening and learning, too. Sue feels this education helped her children become the outstanding, positive, and successful adults they are today.

The University of Houston approved Sue to teach real estate classes on its campus. Sue was thrilled—she was now going to fulfill one of her childhood dreams of being a teacher, even doing so without a college education. The lesson learned here? Never create roadblocks for your dreams. If it is meant to be, there is always a way. Stay positive, work hard, and accept God's miracles as they happen.

Sue was again clueless, this time about how she would teach this class, so she read the entire Principles of Real Estate lesson out loud to the 45 students in her class. During the first session, a few students actually walked out. Sue's mind whirled as she drove home. *I can't do this*, she thought. *The students don't like me, and I don't like them, either.*

She knew something had to change if she was ever going to be an excellent speaker. She needed a technique that would instantly make her feel alive and ready to go. Then, her creative mind began whirling around with ideas, until she came up with the practice of snapping her fingers and repeating, "I'm great…I'm terrific…I'm the best!" The next day, her class went much better, and instead of reading the entire lesson to the students, she switched the roles and had the students read it to her. That day, no one walked out of class.

Later, the college asked Sue to teach the real estate marketing class. One student walked into her class, recognized Sue, and uttered, "Oh, no!" Later, at the break, however, he remarked, "I can't believe you're the same teacher compared to the first class I took with you. What happened?" Sue realized that to accomplish her dreams, she would need to consistently learn and practice. She committed to studying three hours a day, six days a week, a task she carried out for the next 21 years. To this day, Sue still studies one hour a day, six days a week. Ongoing continual learning is critical to personal and professional success.

In 1984, Sue bought out her partners and was the sole owner of her real estate company. Then, two devastating things happened: the housing market spiraled downward, and Sue hit a wall in her battle to lose weight. Can you imagine this woman living in the 1980s, during a time when the media depiction of women was edging toward even more slenderness and even greater height? And Sue was considered neither slender nor tall in stature. The problem with related image distortion is that it can cause depression and anxiety. People may become anxious or depressed if they feel they don't measure up to the ideals they see in the mass media.

This remarkable woman owned her own company, did some public speaking, taught at the University of Houston, and was a leader in the regional real estate franchise. She sat on the board of directors for the Houston Association of Realtors and the Texas Association of Realtors and was the mother to four beautiful children. Now, she thought the only thing lacking was for her to lose weight, and then she would truly have it all.

Sue felt desperate and heard about a psychiatrist who would hypnotize patients to help them lose weight. She immediately called for an appointment. Sue says, "Things didn't go quite as planned, however. The doctor said he couldn't hypnotize me because my mind's thought processes ran too fast, so he prescribed a pill that then made me depressed and so subsequently prescribed medicine for depression." Six months later, Sue was severely depressed and had no memory of work; her condition took a devastating toll on her real estate business. Sue says she had "truly hit rock bottom."

Thankfully, Sue was able to pull herself together enough to discover that the medication prescribed was actually causing her depression. As soon as she quit taking the drug, she began feeling much better.

This brave woman decided to return to the psychiatrist (concealing that she had stopped taking the medication), telling him instead about her ongoing symptoms of depression. Surprisingly, he recommended that she be transported immediately to a psychiatric hospital. She declined the offer and got out of there as quickly as possible. (Today, Sue says, "I should have filed charges against this doctor, preventing him from doing this to others, but at the time I just wasn't strong enough.")

Soon after, Sue's beloved grandmother, the same beautiful person who had loved her unconditionally as a child, died at the age of 87. The next two months, all Sue did was cry for her grandmother, not sure about how to deal with her massive loss. Sue prayed every night that God would help her understand why she had to lose this beloved person. One morning, she remembers hearing an inner voice, a whisper from God, saying, "Do something with your life, and do it now!" Shortly afterward, Sue began her own motivational speaking business, but because she no longer had a successful real estate company, doubt began creeping in again. Sue thought she would not appear credible.

Once again, Sue learned that we can sometimes be our own worst enemy. In all actuality, people generally don't really care about what is going on in your life; what they want is to know how you can help them with what's going on in their lives. Sue knew this was exactly what she wanted to do: help others live the life of their dreams. Sue made the conscious choice to accept herself and use her God-given talents to do what she loved. She merged her real estate company with a good friend's company to become free to pursue her dreams.

Money was tight, and Sue wasn't sure where the next dollar would come from to fund her new business, but she had unwavering faith. Unexpectedly, her mother offered to support her daughter's speaking endeavor for the next six months. This generous offer allowed Sue to get her new business up and running—by joining the National Speakers Association, printing business cards and stationery, and buying a microphone—but more importantly, it made Sue feel accepted. She was not sure if her mother even realized the magnitude of her gift, but that day, Sue began the journey of healing from unresolved childhood wounds, especially feelings of abandonment.

Sue finally realized how exuberant she felt when speaking and helping others, but also how unhappy she was in her marriage. The couple's 27th wedding anniversary was the event that made Sue realize their marriage was finally over, especially after her husband said he was still embarrassed at being seen in public with her. Sue was devastated. Two days later, as she traveled to present "How to Have a Great Day Every Day" to widowed, divorced, and single persons over 55 at the Memorial Presbyterian Church, she heard that whisper again: "God doesn't want you to live like this." By now, her children had left the nest, and there was no better time to tell her husband that she was leaving him.

## TAKE A PAUSE

And just like that, one life chapter was over, and another was about to begin.

Now, Sue would need to get organized to achieve her dreams. The organizational techniques Sue had implemented in her real estate business previously had more than doubled her income. Here was her "aha!" moment: *Maybe I can make money teaching others my technique.*

She had business cards printed, and the same day obtained her first client, making $50 an hour. Sue was excited, and she shared her business news with her mother, but, this time, her mother wasn't as supportive, saying, "You're just a glorified maid." The interesting takeaway here is Sue's external response to others: "No matter what people say, don't let them discourage you."

Sue's new career began to take off. Her client list included such companies as Enron, Ernst and Young, General Dynamics, Dow Chemical, Kellogg Brown and Root, and numerous other businesses in many different industries. The 1990s saw a single Sue go from making $50 an hour to more than $500,000 per year. But this came to an abrupt halt one day as Sue bent over in excruciating pain. She wanted to die to make the pain stop.

Rushed to the emergency room, Sue learned she had a cancerous tumor on one of her kidneys. She took her time to shop around for the best specialist to perform the surgery to remove the tumor and, along with it, her kidney. Before surgery, her doctor asked if she was nervous, and her response was, "Why, no. I have the best doctor, and God will take care of me." Once she turned it over to God, Sue felt complete peace.

As Sue was wheeled out of the recovery room, she overheard the nurses talking about a seminar. She asked who the speaker was and told them about her own time-management class. In the next few minutes, Sue had their business cards, telling her youngest daughter to send them sign-up packages for the class.

Less than six weeks after major surgery, Sue flew with her daughter to Las Vegas, Phoenix, and Cabo San Lucas, Mexico, on business. After returning home, she told her doctor how tired she felt, and he reminded her that she had to take it easy for six months. Sue had only heard the "six" and presumed it meant weeks, not months!

## LIFE IS TIME...MAKE IT COUNT!

It didn't take long before Sue was off and running again, building her company until all three of her girls had come into the business. Things were going great, and then a couple of major detours occurred that changed her business again in a substantial way.

Doctors diagnosed Sue's precious son-in-law, Todd Krampitz, with liver cancer one month after he married her daughter. Everyone focused on helping the couple in every way possible, and Sue traveled the country fulfilling jobs that had already been booked for her daughter. Todd did receive a liver transplant but passed away the following year. Sue sank into a deep depression that lasted almost two years. Her daughter and Todd had been sweethearts since junior high school and now, at only 32, he was gone. It was hard to cope with what her daughter was going through. The lesson learned is that we are not always in control, no matter what happens, we must trust in God.

The second situation occurred when Sue began to realize that over the past few years, her size had started to increase significantly from the waist down. Her first thought, like most women, was that she was merely gaining weight again; however, no matter how hard she tried to diet and exercise, her lower body continued to grow in size.

Startling news came when Sue was diagnosed with lipedema, an inherited chronic genetic disorder of the adipose tissue that generally affects the legs, causing them and sometimes the arms to accumulate massive amounts of fatty tissue. The disease is found in women of all sizes; the excess deposits and expansion of fat cells occur in unusual and particular patterns from the waist to just above the ankle area, with the feet typically spared.

The same woman who had endured years of feeling inferior because of her weight learned that no amount of diet or exercise would correct this disease. This would have stopped most people in their tracks, but not Sue. It only made her more determined to turn this lemon into lemonade—and has she ever served up the lemonade!

It has been 20 years now since Sue's diagnosis, and she still possesses the God-given talent of making others feel special, along with her signature saying: "I'm great! I'm terrific!! I'm the best!!!" She is adored by everyone she meets and a genuine inspiration to others.

Even though she experiences constant pain and uses a wheelchair, this doesn't deter Sue from traveling all over the country to provide her sought-after time-management, organizational, and motivational speaking services. Sue has never given up and never stopped believing in God, no matter the circumstances. Sue is an amazing woman, who is a great inspirational role model.

## SUE'S THOUGHTS ON SUCCESS

*Dream big dreams, then follow up with action, and know in your heart that if it's meant to be, it will happen. Most of all, live an organized life because it's just easier if you do.*
—Sue Pistone

- Identify your strengths and skills.
- Look at your past successes.
- Learn from past experiences.
- Set goals in all areas of your life.
- Use your God-given talents to help others.
- Realize that only you can make you happy.
- You can only change yourself.
- Start and end your day with positive thoughts and actions.
- Keep your life simple.
- Celebrate your life every day, and focus on the good.

## *Write Your Goals for Success*

---
---
---
---
---

(Go to www.GodGaveUsWings.com for a free worksheet.)

## PAY IT FORWARD

Sue's life sets the standard for everyone she meets: "Life Is Time... Make It Count!" She is a beacon of light for those who just can't see past the weeds. She has volunteered for countless committees and nonprofit boards all over the country, sharing her insights on how to generate success. She continues to donate numerous counseling hours toward women-owned entrepreneurs through the Women's Business Enterprise Alliance, the Women's Business Enterprise National Council, the National Speakers Association, and the Todd Krampitz Foundation (TKFoundation.org), which her daughter set up to increase organ donor awareness.

## *List a Few Ways You Can Help Others*

---
---
---
---
---

## BLESSING PRAYER

May God bless your life with abundant love and acceptance from all the people you meet. May God guide you to the person of your dreams, the one who will love you inside and out. May your life lessons be learned quickly and painlessly. May your life be blessed morning, noon, and night with all the best that life can offer. May God keep you in his loving arms, shielding you from life's harsh storms until it's clear to fly again. Amen.

## NEXT CHAPTER

The next story is about a poor Mexican family's desperate quest for survival, taking you on a roller-coaster ride of emotions. A beautiful young lady nicknamed Lilly remembers one of her life's storms more as a blessing than a hardship. Lilly shares how God rained quarters to help feed her family and how having a baby saved her life.

## CHAPTER 4

# The Generational Change

*"See, I am sending an angel ahead of you to guard you along the way and to bring you to the place I have prepared…"*
—Exodus 23:20 (NIV)

## FRONT ROW SEAT

Lilly's narrative will give you a front row view into the lives of three generations of abused women. It will show you how each woman dealt with the devastating effects of abuse in her life and how it affected her children. It will demonstrate the learned behavior of physical violence and its lasting effects, often passed from one generation to another until a brave soul puts a halt to it. In this story, Lilly took control of her life, lifting her face upward and declaring "It stops here!"

The first scene unfolds with the image of Lilly's grandmother enduring lifelong physical abuse at the hands of her husband. Lilly's grandparents lived in severe poverty in a small Mexican border town. Her grandfather reportedly beat her grandmother each time he drank, and the fact that she had given him three girls and no boys seemed to intensify his violent drunken behavior. Lilly's mother remembers growing up wishing she could have protected her mother, often wondering if she had somehow caused the beatings by not being that coveted son. Obviously, this was only her grandfather's weak justification for his horrific behavior: the abuse continued even after Lilly's grandmother gave birth to a son (at which point the husband would say he beat his wife because the child was not his).

Like most abuse, in Lilly's family, it got worse over time. Lilly's now-fragile grandmother attempted suicide, but it wasn't her time to go. Her grandfather's brutal behavior eventually extended to beating his four children. The ongoing cruel behavior seemed to mainly affect Lilly's mother, who began holding hatred in her heart for all men, eventually learning to fight back with a vengeance against anyone getting in her way.

## FEAR ABOUND

The second life scene reveals how Lilly's mother, Jane (not her real name), escaped her abusive father by running away at 17. Jane hooked up with a handsome veteran, who brought her to America. Their non-binding union was short-lived; he soon abandoned Jane and their newly born son. Two years later, the immigrant mother would start working at a meat market and met a man different from all of the others she had known. They quickly fell in love, and he accepted the little boy as his own. Nine months later, Jane would have another child out of wedlock. This time, it was a baby girl. Her official name became Ileana, which means "my God has answered," although she nearly always went by Lilly.

This small family's life was good for a while—until, through fits of jealousy and rage, Jane's inner demons surfaced. Then, just ten months later, she was pregnant again with her third child. Things progressively spiraled out of control, with Lilly's father distancing himself more and more from Jane and the children. Jane's unbridled anger, Lilly recalls, culminated in her mother hitting her dad in the head, gashing it wide open. Outraged and in pain, Lilly's father left, never to return.

Flat broke now with three small children, Jane knew she had to act quickly, or they would soon be homeless. She began working at a bar where her beauty attracted men who fought over her like wild animals. Like so many frightened and abused women, she found herself drawn to the worst of them, a man resembling her vicious father.

## FLASH FROM THE PAST

Mirroring her own mother's life in years past, Jane's new suitor beat her almost daily. She thought about running away, but soon learned she was pregnant with her fourth child. The battery would continue throughout her pregnancy, and the three young children became so frightened of this brute of a man that they began hiding themselves from the potential violence. The oldest child, now seven, would gather up his two siblings at the first sign of conflict and run to a designated closet, where he kept a blanket to crawl under, out of sight. The fighting and yelling turned to weeping then to quiet moans. At this point, it was their clue it was safe to come out. But soon, there was a fourth child, a baby boy, who also needed to be hidden.

Life was nearly unbearable for these small children, either hiding or nursing their mother's severely bruised body back to health. Thank God, the seven-year-old found the strength to soldier on; he seemed to know what to do. The ritual was always the same: find Mother laying on the floor crying covered with bumps and bruises, with her reaching for a painkiller from her stash to ease the pain.

One time was different: the little soldier decided to hunker down no longer and instead emerge, ready for battle, to defend his mother. The little fellow, now eight, knew he needed to arm himself, so he ran to grab an iron frying pan from the kitchen; little did this child realize, he was no match for such a monster. The wicked man took to beating both mother and son. Not until her son was himself battered did Jane find the courage to leave their abusive situation. Now, it was back to the family struggle: no money, no food, and sometimes only a breath away from homelessness. Lilly remembers how her mother would tell them about God, how He was their real Father, who loved them unconditionally, reminding them that He never would ever hurt them.

## ANSWERED PRAYERS

Once again destitute, with not even a nickel for diapers or milk for the baby, Jane knew they needed a miracle. "By the time Mother turned 23 years old," Lilly reports, "she had become a single mother to four little ones. Growing up, Mom had to be tough, strong, and independent, and so she was. Life was harsh, not easy at all, and many times she was left with not even a penny to her name."

> *"Truly I tell you, unless you change and become like little children, you will never enter the kingdom of heaven."*
> —Matthew 18:3 (NIV)

"In desperation," continues Lilly, "I remember she would always make us kneel beside the bed to pray with her. She would tell us, 'God always hears children's prayers because small children are innocent,' and so she was confident that God would answer our prayers. And she was right…our first miracle was a day when we had nothing left to eat; I was about four years old at the time. Mother was crying because she needed formula and diapers for my youngest brother, and she had no money. By now, my older brother and I knew what we had to do…we were to run to the side of our bed and pray, pray for a miracle.

"God answered. As we opened the door to our front porch, we noticed a couple of quarters in the dirt, and then looking around, we found more and more quarters. It was as if someone had sprinkled quarters all over our front yard. We were so happy and excited! We had enough money to buy diapers, formula, tortillas, and a bag of beans to make dinner that night. By now, Mom was crying, but this time they were happy tears because God had heard our prayers. She would always tell us we were not alone; although we might not have a real father present in our lives, we had GOD! We should be happy and give thanks for having the only and very best father in the whole wide world with us always, one who would never leave our side."

Minor miracles such as the "raining of quarters" would keep them alive through this crisis and others over her childhood, but Lilly's real miracle would not come until she was an adult and able to create a life of her own.

"There was a short time in our lives when my mother had no man to cause us pain," notes Lilly. Since her mother had no job skills to support herself and her four children, however, instead of turning to a man, she became involved in a crime ring. Jane was eventually caught and spent several days in jail, leaving the children with a neighbor. The siblings did the only thing they knew in this time of desperation—they prayed every night for their mother to come home. And their prayers were heard. The judge was lenient, sentencing Jane to no additional jail time, but instead, she was given five years of probation and was ordered to pay $300 per month in restitution. Good news, except how was this poverty-stricken woman going to pay $300 monthly, and support her children after being convicted of a felony? Jane made money the only way she knew. The next decade saw Lilly's mother working in a bar again, pushing drinks on men. She would earn three dollars for every man who bought her a drink. Needless to say, this poor woman worked day and night, including cleaning filthy restrooms wiping up human excreta off the floors and walls. It was not a good life, but she had to support her children, and they learned to adapt, they learned to survive, and they learned to do whatever it took to keep their family together.

## WHERE'S MY FATHER?

Lilly and her older brother, now nicknamed "Soldier," took on the brunt of the responsibility of raising each other and their two younger brothers. They cooked, cleaned, and got everyone off to school (on most days). There was very little money for anything outside of the bare necessities, such as school clothes and shoes. They regularly endured taunting by other schoolchildren due to their tattered clothing. Lilly especially remembers the hurtful words because she had to wear her brother's clothes to school. She dreamed of having a beautiful dress and cute shoes like the popular girls—oh, how she envied their lives!

If this wasn't enough, day, after day the children were subjected to demeaning statements surrounding their mother and her job. Lilly often cried herself to sleep, asking God for another life…one with a mother and father…one with food every day…one where she wore girl clothes…but especially a life where she felt safe from the hands of abuse.

After a few years and an expunged criminal record, Jane left the bar scene to work in a warehouse and took a second job in a meat market. Once again, the children were frequently left to their own devices, to raising each other. Her mother brought home what Lilly describes as a "creepy old man to live with us to help pay the rent." Unbeknownst to Jane, this man would turn out to be a sexual predator and would sometimes approach Lilly, threatening to kill her if she told of his abusive behavior. Lilly was still just a little girl, scared and alone. Her only escape from his advances was to run to her mother's room and lock the door to stay out of harm's way, sobbing uncontrollably, begging God repeatedly, "Please help me!" She remembers blaming her father for not being there to protect her, and she began to hate him; she started hating all men, and she began believing—like her mother—that men were born to hurt women.

Lilly recalls that she was told, "God was the only man who would not hurt me! If that was true, why wasn't he answering my prayers? I felted rejected and unheard by God, and I began following in my mother's footsteps of self-loathing." Lilly would later learn that God is love and never the cause of harm, but rather carries us through the pain from the actions of others.

## WHY ME?

Now the third generation affected by abuse. Lilly grew into her teens, meeting a young man with a gentle soul. He was kind to her and would buy her makeup; he wanted her to feel as beautiful on the outside as she was on the inside. No matter how hard he tried, though, Lilly could not erase the years of pain caused by her abuse. She began having fits of jealousy and rage, like her mother. The next thing she knew she had broken up with the only man at the time who had treated her with kindness and asked nothing in return. Lilly began running around with other guys, purposefully drinking and partying to hurt him. To her surprise, he didn't chase after her, but instead decided to move on without her. Lilly felt alone, abandoned, and worthless. Not long after their break-up, she began dating useless men. The first had no job and laid around doing drugs; the second one was abusive when he drank but a real sweetheart when he was sober always telling her how much he loved her.

The partying continued until one day when Lilly and her friends ran into a young man who asked for her telephone number and a date. Sure enough, the following day, Lilly received a call. She hadn't expected him to call, and didn't even recall his name. When he did call, she asked, "What is your name?" Ironically, he shared the same name as Jane's on-and-off boyfriend, a man who repulsed Lilly for the way he treated her mother. Married with children, living a double life, this man pretended to act like a father, something he would never accomplish.

The unpleasant images associated with this young man's name, same as the elder gent, soon faded as he sweet-talked Lilly into their first date. He rapidly swept her off her feet, and six months later—just like her mother—Lilly was pregnant and unmarried. She was now 22, and for the first time, realized she had inherited this lifestyle from her grandmother. *When will it end?* she wondered in desperation.

Jane, meanwhile, was outraged over the pregnancy, calling Lilly every name in the book. She told her she was nothing but a failure and then began filling Lilly's head with notions about the wickedness of men and how "they just love you and leave you." Jane wanted Lilly to raise the baby without a father, and Lilly knew how awful it felt not to have one in her life. This was the last thing she wanted for her child, and she began to panic and started calling the baby's father, asking him to get her out of this mess. Her life had again hit rock bottom. Frantic, she reached out to her Heavenly Father once more: *God, where are you? Don't you see I am lost and in great pain?*

The baby's father, for the time being, remained silent. Feeling lied to and lost, Lilly was, once again, nearly broken. And Jane continued the verbal abuse, whenever possible throwing jabs such as, "What did you expect from a 20-year-old man who never loved you?" Lilly hit bottom! She felt rejected, unloved, and, most of all, like a failure. She went into a deep depression, crying nonstop.

## CHOOSE TO LIVE

*Your life is a gift, with God the Author of your true story. To find the truth in your life's journey, you sometimes need help to cleanse your soul from unwanted graffiti.*

—Connie Rankin

Lilly told her mother she no longer wanted to exist; the emotional pain was too great. Her mother at first looked lost but then began to cry, too. The sight of her daughter pregnant and in such pain was too much for her to bear. Shockingly, Lilly says, her mother turned to her and said, "'We will all take our lives together.' Mother was in so much emotional pain and wanted to end her life, too. She picked up a knife and headed toward my younger brother, saying he would be the first to go, and then, 'You and I will be next. Finally, this will end our suffering,' she said, 'but may God forgive us, for the Bible says we will go to hell if we take our lives.'"

Lilly recalls, "The sight of Mother holding a knife to her wrist scared the heck out of me! I fell to my knees pleading, 'No, Mother, no.' I told her that I loved her too much to see her and my brother die, and what about my unborn child? Surely, it would slowly suffocate once my body was dead, or perhaps worse, live without a mother and father. That moment, I chose to live...and not die. I yelled to my mom to STOP! I took the knife from her, and we held each other tight, sobbing for hours. We decided to keep on going, making the best of what came our way."

"The only way my mother thought she could go on, though, was if she could dull the pain. She began taking pills to help ease her suffering, but it was always there, just waiting to expose itself. She started taking more and more pills until it became an addiction."

## CHANGE THE MESSAGE

*A positive attitude gives you power over your circumstances instead of your circumstance having power over you~*
—Anonymous

After this episode in Lilly's life, things began changing for the better. Her best friend got her a job at the company where she'd worked for over two years. Lilly started hearing positive messages from the people at her workplace; they complimented her, telling her how much they appreciated her hard work. Gradually, Lilly started feeling valuable and more confident.

Soon afterward, Lilly would welcome her new baby boy into the world, calling him an answer to her prayers. The child's father stepped up and decided to be a part of their lives, and things seemed good, at least on the surface. She and the baby moved in with the father in their own apartment. Things were looking up, but Lilly could not accept the blessing. She hung on tightly to the victim mentality, and Jane's echoing words that she would be "a sorry mother."

Lilly was so blinded by the hurt and pain in her past that she sometimes failed to see that the young man standing beside her had become a loving and caring father and helpmate. She thought that since he'd hurt her once, he would do it again. This man was different from all the rest because he only wanted to erase her pain and promised to love her with every breath in his being. And he did. He became her rock, giving her strength and encouragement each time she fell, reminding her to believe in herself. Lilly would fall and stumble many times but learned how to get back up stronger than before. This precious man fiercely protected her and his son, treating Lilly like no man in her past. Standing by her through life's tribulations, their love grew stronger. He was the one who would not abandon her. He would become her life partner and her soulmate. And yet, something was still missing.

Slowly but surely, Lilly's life changed because Lilly began to change from the inside out. Various earth angels along the way gave her messages of hope, love, and encouragement. She felt God's presence: "God clearly spoke to me, saying 'My child, I never left you; it was you who had your back toward me all along. You have allowed hate and pain to foreshadow the many blessings I have in store for your life. I tried to catch you many times, but you were consumed more with life than with Me. You missed many opportunities to speak up and be heard, instead of allowing fear to consume your very soul.' God told me it was up to me to open my heart and forgive all those who had wronged me because one day they would answer to a greater power."

One year later, Lilly realized that by changing her thoughts she could change her life and the lives of those around her. Five years into their relationship, her now-husband followed her footsteps to God as he learned to trust and have faith. With every obstacle, they stopped and prayed as a couple. Before long, Lilly was more positive, happier, and, bit by bit, less frightened of the world. She later learned another useful phrase for her life, words passed down to a friend from her fourth-grade teacher: "Can't never could do anything." "What a lovely gift to give someone," Lilly says, "and I have shared it with many others." Her newest tool is when she begins to stray toward fear, she asks herself, *Where is this coming from?* It guides Lilly toward the root of the fear, to understand how to change fear into faith.

Everyone has a story. Regardless of ethnic group, economic status, or age, everyone has one. Some stories are so horrific that we witness spirits completely broken; one wonders how anyone can emotionally survive such ordeals. Perhaps surprisingly, this has more to do with how one chooses to remember their past. The major difference in the stories you've heard is presentation "how the storyteller tells their story." Some people tell their stories from the standpoint of fear and blame, some even from hatred. The ones coming from love and faith perspectives exhibit the most hope and herald the most positive change.

Stories framed in love and forgiveness provide great hope that all things are possible. Stories framed in fear, blame, or hatred, however, tend to flip a "not my fault, nothing I can do" switch, making one feel as if it's pointless to try to fly— even if she or he has flown in the past.

> *The past is where you learned the lesson…the future is where you apply the lesson…and the present is for living! If you can apply this motto to your life's decree, you have a good chance of soaring with other eagles.*
>
> —Connie Rankin

Lilly is in her second year of college at Houston Community College majoring in business and is a licensed real estate agent. She took charge of her life, realizing God does not make mistakes, and as her mother said, "God is always with you and will never leave you." Lilly's brave act "it stops here" has changed her life, and will for generations to come.

## LILLY'S THOUGHTS ON SUCCESS
- You are in control of your own destiny.
- You are no longer a victim.
- Choose to accept or reject others people's behaviors.
- You are in control of your feelings.
- Rise above negativity.
- You no longer need to own the misery and sorrow of the past.
- Change your actions today to change your future. Use "cancel" to rid yourself of negative thoughts, replacing them with positive ones.

- Ask yourself, *Where is the fear coming from?*
- Replace fear with faith, and know that you are not alone.

## Write Your Goals for Success

_____

_____

_____

_____

(Go to www.GodGaveUsWings.com for a free worksheet.)

## PAY IT FORWARD

Lilly has paid it forward, many times over, through her thoughtfulness and generosity showed to others. Her heart is filled with an abundance of love that pours out kind words of encouragement to everyone she meets. Lilly exemplifies one who flies in God's glory.

## List a Few Ways You Can Help Others

_____

_____

_____

_____

## DEPRESSION HURTS, AND DOMESTIC VIOLENCE WOUNDS (OR WORSE)

Here is your call to action: If you (or someone you know) are depressed, seek help. Untreated, depression often gets worse and may lead to suicide attempts that, unfortunately, may be successful. Also, unfortunately, people at times attempt to treat themselves in manners not conducive to healing. Depression can be a vicious cycle, but help is out there—and *you* can be the change!

Please, should you find yourself a victim of domestic violence, or if you are a survivor seeking help to cope with the effects of abuse—even if you have left the abuser or were abused as a child—contact a local domestic violence support group or make an appointment with a therapist trained in treating abuse. Remember, abuse is a crime in all 50 states. Especially if your abuse is ongoing, contact your local women's shelter; they will provide you with information to help lead you to safety and with counseling concerning your legal rights.

According to HealthyPlace.com, Lilly's family traits are those described as battered woman syndrome, which is brought about by domestic violence toward women (and children). Effects of this syndrome may include the following:

- Becoming violent themselves, especially in response to threats
- Suicide attempts
- Use of drugs and abuse of alcohol
- Development of eating disorders
- Self-abuse
- Anxiety and depression
- Headaches
- Poor social skills
- Entering into an abusive relationship at some point (often seen with abused children)
- Nightmares
- Sleep troubles (such as insomnia)
- Back and pelvic pain
- Gastrointestinal disturbances
- Generalized chronic pain
- Mental health problems (such as post-traumatic stress disorder)

## BLESSING PRAYER

My prayer is that you know God loved you enough to have made you in His likeness for greatness. You are a unique person with special talents given to you to fulfill His great plan for the life only you can pursue. May God bless you and show you how you can be all things if you believe. I can…I will! Amen.

## NEXT CHAPTER

The next chapter will have you on the edge of your seat while reading the adventure of a cute little Southern girl with long curly blonde hair. She knew at age 15 that she wanted to serve her country, especially after 9/11, but first, she had to grow up. This young woman would trade in her dancing shoes for combat boots to become the female version of Rambo.

## CHAPTER 5

# Hope for the Future

*The two most important days in your life are the day you are born, and the day you find out why.*
—Mark Twain

## A WARRIOR'S EARLY DAYS

W ho could have guessed that a cute little Southern girl named Kendra, with long curly blonde hair, would later grow up to become the Army's female version of Rambo? Kendra Coleman lived in Jackson, Georgia, a town with a population of less than 61,000. Before graduating from Luella High School, she enjoyed soccer, basketball, track, and martial arts, but she especially loved hip-hop choreography dance.

Life was not always easy for Kendra growing up. She came from a broken home; her father left when she was just seven years old. Her mother had to work two jobs just to make ends meet. This required young Kendra and her little brother to look after themselves most of the time.

Remarkably, this young girl knew at age 15 that she wanted to serve her country, especially after 9/11, but first, she had to grow up. Like most teenagers at the time, she loved hip-hop music and was thrilled when, in a fortuitous encounter, she was asked to be a backup dancer for a band. Wow! Can you imagine how excited this girl must have felt to be paid to dance?

Then, in 2007, after turning 18, she traded in her dance career for the U.S. Army. How does a young woman go from full-blown girly girl to being one of the few military police paratroopers, graduating airborne school at age 20, and becoming one of the youngest female Army sergeants?

Kendra's early military experience actually started out more like the 1980s movie *Private Benjamin*, about a clueless young woman, played by Goldie Hawn, who joins the U.S. Army on a whim and finds herself in a more difficult situation than she ever expected.

Let's take a look into Kendra's childhood to see how it shaped who she is today. Her earliest memory involves her parents getting a divorce when she was in second grade. She remembers her dad pulling her out of class the day of the divorce. He wanted to explain to his young daughter why she wouldn't see him for a while...what Kendra didn't realize was that he actually meant for many, many years. Shortly thereafter, her dad moved to Colorado, leaving this young girl crying and wondering most of her life, *Why did Daddy leave me?*

The sudden departure of her father forced Kendra's mother to work long hours for them to survive. Her mother knew that if she were ever to provide a better life for her family, she would need to further her education. This brave mother decided to enroll in nursing school to become a registered nurse. As you can imagine, it was tough for this woman going to school while working a full-time job. It was not an easy decision to leave her children alone, fending for themselves, but this sacrifice was for their future.

One of Kendra's fondest childhood memories involved her saving a little wiry-haired puppy from drowning in a muddy lake. She remembers spotting this small creature from afar, struggling to free himself from sludge covering his tiny body. Kendra knew she needed to act fast if the puppy was to survive. She began trudging through the waist-deep mud until she finally reached the other side. Kendra quickly grabbed the pup, clenching him tightly in her arms until they were safely back on shore. She named her new best friend, Benji. Little did she know that his new name meant "son"—son of the right hand, son of the south—and he was all that to Kendra for the next 10 years of his life.

Shortly afterward, Kendra's mother met a man named Greg, with whom she would remain in a long-term relationship. For a while, Greg would help fill the void of Kendra's absent father. However, this couple would eventually break up, shattering Kendra's heart with the feeling of losing yet another father.

## THE MISSING LINK

> *But the Advocate, the Holy Spirit, whom the Father will send in my*
> *name, will teach you all things and will remind you of everything…*
> —John 14:26 (NIV)

Like most children, Kendra gravitated toward the missing link in her life: time. Her father was gone, and her mother had to work, leaving little time for her children. Naturally, this made Kendra want to hang out at her best friend's house, where there was a model mom who was always home with her children, unlike Kendra's.

Kendra was an impressionable teenager when her mother met her second boyfriend, Jerry Ray, in nursing school. Kendra's description of him actually sounds more like Superman! He was in the Army, a parachuter, firefighter, helping save lives. Kendra says, "Jerry Ray is a religious man who believes in God and who has such an amazing soul." He was everything Kendra wanted in a father—loving, motivated, responsible, and disciplined, a man she looked up to, even to this day.

This new union between her mother and Jerry Ray resulted in her family moving to Henry County, to a much bigger city just south of Atlanta. Kendra switched high schools at age 15 and was there until graduating from Luella High School in 2007.

During Kendra's senior year, she began working part-time at Hooters, and this is where she met an up-and-coming group called the Ying Yang Twins, out of Atlanta. The group invited Kendra and her friend to check out one of their shows. The next thing you know, Kendra had left Hooters to join the group as a backup dancer, where she got to do what she loved most...hip-hop dance.

However, after traveling a year with the group, she realized that the job was primarily based on looks, and youth doesn't last forever. She wanted to do something different...something more fulfilling... something more like Jerry Ray.

Kendra truly admired this man as a father figure and decided to make a drastic decision: to join the military. However, Jerry Ray was stationed overseas, and nobody took this cute little teenager in four-inch heels seriously. Kendra's life quickly changed.

## THE DEVELOPMENT OF LADY RAMBO

*To regret one's own experiences is to arrest one's own development.*
*To deny one's own experiences is to put a lie into the lips of one's own*
*life. It is no less than a denial of the soul.*
—Oscar Wilde

One day, unexpectedly, she showed up at the military recruiting office wearing her stilettos shoes and carrying a little furry purse, to enlist in the Marine Corps. Imagine what those Marines must have thought to see this cute little teenage girl.

They tried to quash her enthusiasm by having her come back the next day at six a.m. Instead, it made Kendra more determined. She arrived bright and early, eager to join, but no one was there. She waited...and waited...for hours, believing it was only a test. She finally gave up after waiting four hours but did not abandon the idea of joining. Instead, Kendra headed upstairs to the Army recruiting center; this time, she was taken seriously and was signed up on the spot. Kendra left with a big smile on her face, not realizing the magnitude of her decision. Her smile later turned to frantic tears.

Kendra was given a packet of information but was too excited to worry about the detailed instructions. Her only interest was in the map for possible army locations. As you may have guessed, Hawaii was her first choice.

This young girl was truly clueless. She had no one to guide her—not her absent father, not her father figure—who was deployed to Afghanistan. No one.

When it was time for Kendra to report to basic training, this totally clueless girl showed up wearing only the clothes on her back—tight jeans, girly knee-high boots, eyeliner—and toting her furry little purse. She got off the bus and was told to go check in, where she was given her physical training (PT) uniform, consisting of a gray T-shirt and black shorts. That was it. No shoes, no socks, no undergarments—for three days.

Can you imagine how silly she must have felt in her PT uniform wearing her girly boots? Not surprisingly, Kendra's situation grew progressively worse. She was forced to wear her fashion boots to run two miles every day for the next three days. As if boot camp wasn't tough enough, add cute suede boots, and you've got a moving target. The drill sergeants showed no mercy, laughingly calling her "Private Boots," among other slurs.

Thank goodness, the Army finally gave Kendra a $500 advance to buy herself the necessities, like underwear, socks, and the appropriate shoes, until official boot camp started.

Two weeks later, the reality set in regarding the magnitude of her decision. Desperate, she began calling her mother every chance she got, crying and pleading for her mother to find a way to get her out. Kendra asked her mom, "Can't you just tell them I didn't know what I was doing…that I made a *big* mistake?" It must have been terrible for Kendra's mother to hear her baby girl's emotional pleas for help, especially knowing there was little she could do. Every call to her mother was a cry for help: "Please, Mom, get me out or help me escape…please get me out of here…please."

Just as Kendra thought life couldn't get any worse…she was wrong. She was paired up with a rebellious battle buddy, whose mouthiness would result in disciplinary actions for both of them to endure, including a multitude of push-ups and sit-ups and runs for several miles, over and over again, for two agonizing months, until her battle buddy was finally kicked out of the Army. Kendra later realized this dreadful woman actually did her a favor; because of the additional exercise, she began outperforming most of the guys in their rigorous training program.

*Courage doesn't always roar. Sometimes courage is the quiet voice at the end of the day saying, I will try again tomorrow.*
—Mary Ann Radmacher

Finally, Kendra's lucky break—realizing she was there for the duration—made her change her mindset by asking herself what her idol, Jerry Ray, would do. She began setting daily goals for herself. It wasn't easy, but she gradually started looking forward to the daily routine of learning new battle techniques.

Kendra's Armed Services Vocational Aptitude Battery test results indicated a high aptitude for the military police; this field was her first choice because of the combat assignments. This young woman was now the Army's female version of G.I. Joe, pushing herself to the next level. Kendra was later recognized as one of only 10 people out of 120 soldiers earning the title "Best of the Best," allowing for special privileges. She graduated at the top of her class and was later to train as a paratrooper. All she knew was that after seeing the Army's cool video, she wanted to wear the maroon beret, not focusing on the fact that it was an international symbol of elite airborne forces.

Kendra realized that the military's intention was to break her down to build her back up stronger, more capable, and more disciplined, and these were the same traits she admired in Jerry Ray.

Kendra says, "At the end of the day, no matter how hard it was, I celebrated graduation with honors." She remembers laughingly saying to her mother, "You finally showed up!"

It was then time for Kendra to report to her duty station for three weeks of hardcore airborne training in Fort Benning, a U.S. Army post outside Columbus, Georgia. This post proudly introduces itself online as having the "Best Soldiers, Leaders, and Families in the Army!"

It was time for airborne graduation. Remember that Kendra's primary focus was receiving the maroon beret, but instead, she received her blood wings, an airborne tradition. This painful ritual involves an instructor or comrade of the graduate receiving the parachutist badge placing the pin of the badge pointing toward the chest of the graduate, then slamming it against the graduate's chest, resulting in the pin being driven into the flesh.

Just imagine how disappointed this 18-year-old must have felt, not learning until graduation that she wouldn't get a maroon beret until being stationed in an airborne unit. Kendra said, "I had endured the extensive training, jumping out of airplanes, constantly running in army boots, and then enduring bloody pinning, to later find out: No maroon beret. You've got to be kidding me…Well, at least, I'll be stationed in Hawaii."

Kendra and her new Army buddy were sent home pending their orders, the only two females graduating airborne school without orders. It took about a week before her orders were posted online. As the excitement built, it quickly was crushed when she read "Germany," not "Hawaii." "No…No…This must be wrong." Kendra immediately called the Army's Human Resources department to tell them about the mistake: "I picked Hawaii as my first choice, not Germany."

They assured her it was no mistake. Kendra began to freak out, crying and repeatedly saying, "Oh, my god!"

Okay, now what?

Kendra was scared to death to go to Germany. So instead of going alone, she decided to quietly get married to her high school sweetheart rather than going solo to a foreign land. She would later regret this impetuous decision.

Kendra's biggest fear became her reality: she was deployed to Germany alone. It took over six months of red tape before Kendra's husband could join her in Germany—shortly thereafter, the newlyweds decided to call it quits—and her soon to be ex-husband headed home for the United States.

In less than a year, this teenage girl had joined the Army, become a paratrooper, got married, gone to Germany, and got a divorce, all before her 19th birthday. This young GI was stationed in Germany's Special Troops Battalion, the military's higher echelon brigade, a division of the U.S. Army Military Police, which she loved.

Kendra was later disheartened to go from the military police to operations as the first sergeant's personal driver. Later, she was assigned to the arms room to keep track of the entire armory, which was a big job for a 20-year-old. True to form, Kendra's goal was to organize this disheveled mess and make it into an award-winning armory, which she did in less than a year.

During Kendra's assignment in Germany, her platoon went through rigorous training in preparation for their upcoming deployment to Afghanistan. Kendra heard horror stories about how some other soldiers were injured and remember one in particular, about a male soldier losing both his legs in a vehicle bomb blast. Interestingly, Kendra's legs began tingling after hearing this horrific story. She thought, "What would I do in such a blast?"

Kendra wondered if her initial physical reaction had been a premonition, a compassionate response, or both. Either way, the next 10 months, she would train in case of such a catastrophe, to save herself and others.

## INFINITE WISDOM

*Even though I walk through the darkest valley, I will fear no evil, for you are with me; your rod and your staff, they comfort me.*
—Psalm 23:4 (NIV)

In November 2009, Kendra's 173rd Airborne Brigade was deployed to assist in the war in Afghanistan. The war had assumed a higher global profile in 2009, as Taliban attacks increased inside Pakistan. U.S. and NATO troop levels in Afghanistan rose above 100,000, most of them American, and Kendra was now one of them.

Kendra was stationed in Logar Province, Afghanistan, the primary operation known as Forward Operating Base (FOB) Shank. It was the Police Academy, led by a U.S. Police Mentoring Training team to train local Afghan National Police. Kendra's assignment remained as her first sergeant's driver. The rest of her platoon was stationed in a much more hellish environment known as Combat Outpost (COP) Charkh, a much smaller military camp located in a small Afghanistan village, to protect the villagers.

Most people would have preferred the main FOB Shank, allowing for showers every day, with hot meals and a safe place to sleep. Not Kendra. She felt guilty about living what she calls "the high life" in contrast to the rest of her platoon. They were enduring daily enemy warfare, living in makeshift tents with no showers for almost a month, until they went back to FOB Shank for supplies.

Kendra felt she was trained for combat, not as a driver, and wanted to be with her battle buddies, no matter the cost. Kendra pleaded with her first sergeant daily for over a month for a reassignment...until it finally happened.

Kendra got her wish and was subsequently reunited with her 173rd Platoon in COP Charkh, as a military police officer. This region was one of the most dangerous locations in Eastern Afghanistan, just north of the city of Gardez. There were 127 soldiers (125 men and 2 women) in her troop, whose mission was to train the Afghan police and protect the local villagers.

Sadly, Kendra could not always trust the Afghan police, the local villagers, or even the young children. The Taliban would either bribe or convince locals to fire upon or use homemade bombs against the U.S. soldiers.

On April 4, 2010, after Kendra's reassignment, she was traveling in the back of a high-mobility multipurpose wheeled vehicle when an improvised explosive device (IED) exploded, severely crushing the driver's legs. Kendra pulled the soldier from the driver's seat and applied life-saving tourniquets to both legs. Remarkably, Kendra survived, suffering only a minor concussion with cuts and bruises. She wondered, *Was this the event related to the premonition from 10 months earlier?*

Life was not easy for anyone living in the midst of a battlefield, a terrible scene of death and destruction surrounded by mistrust and constant gunfire. Kendra, like the rest of her platoon, lived in makeshift tents and slept on rickety bunk beds. She slept in full uniform, with a gun resting on her chest. The Islamic call to prayer woke the U.S. soldiers at 4:30 a.m. every day over a loudspeaker, blasting the morning recitation.

Fortunately, her first sergeant was meticulous about safety and enforced extensive "what if" training for any unforeseen emergency. Kendra said that this type of preparation training increased the survival rate of his troops a hundredfold compared to other combat outposts. His troops were required to wear safety goggles and earplugs and to carry a tourniquet in their left pants pocket.

Kendra's platoon survived the bitter winter months to now endure the Afghani summer, with squelching heat reaching 100 degrees in May. The temperature did not stop the Taliban's villainous attacks of gunfire and explosives from every direction. The soldiers' survival required them to wear full-body combat gear, including bulletproof vests, 24/7.

It was May 11, 2010, when Kendra's commander received a call from the Afghani police about finding an IED. This prompted her squad leader to gather up soldiers to investigate and secure the IED before detonation.

The team leader told Kendra she did not have to go, but she said that if the rest of the team was going, she would, too.

Kendra's team headed out on foot to find and secure the IED. All of the sudden, she felt an overwhelming sense of evil in the air, and she knew something bad was about to happen. Her chest tightened, her heart began pounding, and her stomach was in knots. All Kendra's senses had heightened—hearing, smell, sight—she felt more alert and even noticed that the clouds seemed a little grayer than usual.

Apparently, Sergeant Hon felt something, too, because he changed the route toward the bazaar. Instead of using the more direct path, he made a detour, taking his platoon the long way around, climbing over walls, crawling in muddy ditches, and crossing a river, all to prevent a possible ambush.

Kendra's team finally reached the bazaar, which was emptier than usual. Only two guys were standing next to a water well house and 10 soldiers from Kendra's squad. The soldiers split up, walking in a staggered formation, to check for any suspicious sightings in the random side trails lined with houses and little stores. Then, the squad formed a zigzag approach to prevent the possibility of the enemy from taking out the entire team, to limit casualties. Out of the 10 soldiers, there were only two women: Kendra and a medic.

The village was eerily quiet…not a sound other than the rustling noise of footsteps belonging to the armed soldiers.

Kendra looked down an alleyway and saw three suspicious men. When they saw the soldiers, they took off running. Kendra began announcing what she saw to her squad leader in front of her—"Alley clear…Man praying…Road clear"—then Kendra had a strong urge to get off the roadway, especially since she was coming up on a blind corner. Kendra stepped up on a narrow two-foot ledge and began hugging the wall.

Just as she reached the corner, she looked down with her weapon drawn to make sure everything was clear before moving forward; Kendra remembers that, while hugging the wall, she saw a random pile of tires, then she heard a loud explosion.

Everything began to move in slow motion. After the blast, Kendra remembers thinking, *Oh my God. One of my battle buddies got hit!* She started falling toward the ground…seeing pieces of airborne flesh whirling in the air.

Kendra remembers asking herself repeatedly, "Who got hit?"

As she was falling, she thought again about how the tires were out of place. Was the bomb hidden in the pile? Kendra saw her sergeant in front of her and then knew it wasn't him who'd been hit. So, who? *Oh, My God! Who got hit by the bomb?*

Kendra was on the ground, seeing flesh and blood all around her when she finally realized that she was the one hit. No one else. Just her. She knew the drill from just a month earlier. She reached in her left pants pocket for her tourniquet, but it was gone. She had no other choice than to apply pressure using both hands to her left leg to stop the bleeding.

She knew it was time to assess her injuries. Kendra first tried moving the toes on her right foot—good, they moved—then the left…nothing. It was time to implement the Army's emergency five-minute war pause— stop, look, listen—to immediately assess the current situation.

By this point, Kendra knew she had been severely hurt, as she continued to clench the remains of her left leg. The medic immediately came to her aid, wrapping two tourniquets around the upper portion of Kendra's leg to stop the bleeding. Kendra asked if she had lost her leg, and the medic told her she was going to be okay. Kendra again asked, "I've lost my leg?" The same response: "You're going to be fine."

Kendra kept asking, "I've lost my leg? I've lost my leg?" Always getting the same response: "No, no, no, you didn't. You are going to be fine." But, all the while, Kendra knew the horrible truth.

This part of Kendra's story is difficult for her to share and difficult for this civilian to hear, especially since Kendra suffers from post-traumatic stress disorder (PTSD). This serious condition can develop after experiencing a traumatic or terrifying event. PTSD is a lasting consequence of traumatic ordeals that causes intense fear, helplessness, and horror.

After just a few minutes, this remarkable young woman was ready to resume her story. Kendra says that she wants to show others that what doesn't kill you can make you stronger; it's your decision. I realized at that moment, talking to Kendra, that this is what real courage looks like. Blaine Lee Pardoe best defines it: "Courage is holding on one minute longer than everyone else. Courage is stepping forward when every fiber of your being says step back. Courage is being willing to do the impossible because it is the right thing to do." Kendra remembers, as she lay on the dirt road in the middle of Afghanistan, wishing that she was anywhere else but there. There was heavy gunfire all around her while she helplessly lay there with no weapon to defend herself, at the total mercy of her battle buddies.

Kendra kept closing her eyes, believing mentally she could escape the horror, but her medic knew differently and kept slapping her face to keep her engaged. Kendra was transported by stretcher to a grassy area and left in the field for a brief moment, until the soldiers could secure the area. Meanwhile, another soldier shot up a flare, indicating their location for the helicopter to land, but the sparks from the flare set the field on fire, preventing the planned rescue.

The situation rapidly deteriorated, with blazing fire approaching the confined Kendra—still strapped to the gurney. Somehow, this woman mustered up the strength to use her uninjured leg to push herself across the grassy field until she was out of harm's way.

Shortly thereafter, Sergeant Hon ran over to grab hold of the stretcher to carry Kendra to safety.

Even though Kendra was in shock from her horrific injury, she knew things were going horribly wrong. She kept asking, "Are you sure we are not going to catch on fire here?" and "Have I lost my leg?" Repeatedly. The response was always the same: "You are going to be fine." Then, Sergeant Hon spoke up to calm Kendra by saying, "Private Coleman, before you know it, you will be up playing soccer again."

There was no place left to land the helicopter in that dangerous war zone being besieged by gunfire. Instead, the safest thing to do was for the helicopter to hoist Kendra up 100 feet into the air while the soldiers stood guard.

It sounds simple, but apparently, in haste, Kendra's stretcher was incorrectly connected, and halfway up, it began spinning out of control from the wind generated by the helicopter's propellers.

In just one day, this unfortunate girl endured a life-threatening injury, a blazing fire, and being knocked unconscious from a twirling baton-like gurney!

Once on the helicopter, she regained consciousness and believed she was finally safe. She was transported back to FOB Shank, where she was greeted by all of her team members. Only Kendra would sit up on the gurney to give everyone a thumbs-up while fixing her hair.

The army immediately flew Kendra to Bagram, the largest U.S. military base in Afghanistan, where she stayed for only 24 hours. Kendra's hair was so matted from blood that the nurses made the decision to shave her head. Kendra was horrified with the news and began crying hysterically: "My leg...now my hair!" Thankfully, a fellow soldier's wife heard the terrible news and drove five hours to be by Kendra's bedside. She then volunteered for the painstaking task of combing out the desiccated blood until Kendra's hair could be partially washed, saving her hair. At the time, Kendra thought that if she lost her hair, she wouldn't be cute anymore, especially after losing her leg.

Sometimes, you wonder just how much a human being can take, then you realize that this girl has true moxie to survive such a horrendous ordeal.

Kendra realized that people were looking at her strangely when they came to visit, and she decided to look at herself in a mirror. Shockingly, her reflection revealed a person whose eyes resembled a dark hole: the whites of her eyes were completely black because of the massive explosion. Kendra was mortified to have been talking to people looking like this...only Kendra.

However, because Kendra wore safety goggles at the time of the explosion, her eyes would return to their normal beautiful brown color.

On May 14, 2010, Kendra arrived at Walter Reed Hospital in Washington, DC. This was the U.S. Army's flagship medical center from 1909 to 2011, the largest military medical center in the United States. It was the first destination in caring for the wounded from conflicts around the world.

Upon arrival, Kendra was in the intensive care unit, and her parents flew in from Georgia to be by her side, including her hero, Jerry Ray, who had left his military post, driving days to get to the hospital. Kendra was relieved when she saw Jerry Ray because she knew he would know what to do—and she was right.

Family and friends rotated shifts, sitting with Kendra 24/7 for the next 22 days while she was hooked up to a multitude of IVs. Her family tried to console Kendra by telling her everything would be all right. Jerry Ray was different; his impactful message came from a fellow soldier: "When a soldier goes through an injury of this magnitude they have two choices: climb or fall. It's your choice, Airborne. It's *your* choice."

These words, "climb or fall," resonated with Kendra, and on the 23rd day, she asked the doctors, "What do I have to do to get out of the hospital into outpatient housing?" The answer? A laborious eight-step process involving getting off of the 10 IVs and using a wheelchair, crutches, walker, the prosthetic limb and one crutch, cane, and finally, solely walking with the prosthetic.

Now that Kendra knew the process, she set a new goal. She decided to eliminate something every day. After just two months, Kendra was walking on her new prosthetic limb, although it would take two years for complete rehabilitation. After two months, her parents had to go back to work; Troy, her younger brother, was flown in to stay with her for the next year during rehab.

This girl may have lost a limb, but she didn't lose her sense of humor.

Kendra recalls a time when she told her 18-year-old brother, while they were at the hospital to take her first steps on her own, to walk in front of her like a girl, shaking his hips with a sway; she wanted to see how girls were supposed to walk—especially the sway. Little did Kendra know that a female general was walking just behind them, until the general burst out laughing, saying, "Please do...I have to see this." Luckily, since Troy wasn't in the military, he could decline both Kendra's and the general's requests.

Seriously, Kendra did wonder how she would ever be soft and delicate again while wearing a hard prosthetic limb. Surprisingly, almost immediately, Ross Perot began calling Kendra almost daily after reading about her plight. He would say, "Kendra, can you walk yet? As soon as you can, I am going to fly you to Oklahoma City to work with the best specialist," and after 10 months, she was ready.

Some of you may ask, "Who is Ross Perot?" He is an American businessman best known for being an independent presidential candidate in 1992 and the Reform Party presidential candidate in 1996.

Perot has owned several businesses and had an estimated net worth of about $3.5 billion in 2012. He is ranked by Forbes as the 134th richest person in the United States.

This kind and generous man lived up to his promise and paid for Kendra to have two custom-made prosthetics, costing $40,000 each. He then paid all of her living expenses while in Oklahoma City to work with Scott Sabolich, the leader in prosthetics. Sabolich designed, for the first time, a prosthetic limb that Kendra could wear in her stilettos shoes.

Kendra was the first amputee to walk in four-inch heels again; this girl got her sway back.

Surprisingly, Kendra's intention was to get back out to battle with her platoon in Afghanistan. Once Kendra realized this wasn't possible, she set a new goal: to graduate from college and to become a sergeant. To help her accomplish such a goal, her college professor drove more than 20 minutes each way to the hospital every day until Kendra got caught up with her classwork and was ready for her final exam.

Kendra graduated from college with a bachelor's degree in business management and applied her degree toward making sergeant. Once she completed this goal, she set another: to go back to Germany to greet her platoon and say their final goodbyes.

Kendra could have taken an earlier medical discharge but elected instead to complete the full five years and receive her honorable medical discharge with her fellow platoon members. She was awarded several medals, including two Purple Hearts, an Army Achievement Medal, and a Combat Action Badge.

## CIVILIAN TRANSITION

Now a civilian, she got married in 2011 to Anthony, a fellow Army soldier. They both got jobs in Houston and eventually settled down in nearby Katy, Texas. In 2013, Kendra became pregnant, and they decided to move back to Jackson, Georgia, where she had a family to help. She is now the mother of a precious little girl.

About Ross Perot, Kendra says, "He has taken me under his wing and has been an excellent mentor in my life." She's also met First Lady Michelle Obama and former First Lady Laura Bush, both whom she describes as "really nice."

## SUCCESS

In the meantime, Kendra is a national motivational speaker, sharing how, just when she thought her life was over, it had just begun. She regularly appears on national TV and in the news. She hopes to motivate others to never to give up and says, "Don't let the enemy determine your future—improvise and overcome."

Kendra continues to speak at different Ross Perot–hosted events, in Las Vegas, New York, and Washington, DC, and at other corporate events. She especially enjoys speaking at various schools and women's groups.

## KENDRA'S THOUGHTS ON SUCCESS

- You always have a choice in life; you can be either a victim or a victor.
- Change your attitude, and you will change your life.
- Don't let others' negativity affect your future.
- Listen to your inner voice.
- Accept help from others.
- Find a mentor to guide you on the roads not yet traveled.
- Follow through with your goals.
- Learn to be your best advocate.
- Find your joy, and you will find your purpose.
- Don't let the enemy determine your future—improvise and overcome.

## *Write Your Goals for Success*

_____

_____

_____

_____

_____

(Go to www.GodGaveUsWings.com for a free worksheet.)

## PAY IT FORWARD

This veteran volunteers regularly to speak at high schools and colleges, sharing her powerful message of how to climb, and not fall, and how that's your decision.

Sometimes, people come into your life for a single reason, and other times, the reason is multipurpose, gradually unfolding until you realize it's bigger than you could have ever imagined.

Who could have known that on May 6, 2015, after completing my interview with Kendra in Savannah, Georgia, I would soon hear the dreadful news that my mother had passed away unexpectedly in her sleep? I was devastated and fell to my knees sobbing. Kendra reached down and picked me up to console me. I didn't realize the magnitude of her action until later that night, when it hit me that Kendra was not wearing her prosthetics that day. I realized that it's Kendra's second nature to help others, as she had done so many times before.

## *List a Few Ways You Can Help Others*

_____

_____

_____

_____

## BLESSING PRAYER

May God bless you with the needed courage to overcome life's obstacles and strengthen your wings to bravely soar at altitudes that take your breath away, and may you find your true essence of joyful living. Amen.

## NEXT CHAPTER

This story will give you a glimpse back in history to a beautiful child raised by second-generation Japanese-American farmers, who almost lost their heritage and identity because of false assumptions that they were the enemy. Her story demonstrates how her craving for equality helped her become a woman of genuineness and how she helped everyone else in the process.

## CHAPTER 6

# Who Am I?

*Now to him who is able to do immeasurably more than all we ask
or imagine, according to his power that is at work within us...*
—Ephesians 3:20 (NIV)

## FINDING HER WAY

Imagine being of Japanese descent and living in America after
World War II, the deadliest conflict in human history. The
war began on September 1, 1939, and ended six years later, in
September 1945. Although the killing ceased, the Cold War began
almost immediately afterward and lasted throughout most of the
remainder of the twentieth century.

Over 127,000 citizens of the United States were imprisoned
during World War II. The crime? Their Japanese ancestry. In February

1942, President Roosevelt signed an executive order dictating that all Japanese-Americans living on the West Coast relocate to internment camps. Japanese-Americans living in other parts of the country were not allowed to travel more than 2 miles from where they lived without FBI approval. Community leaders were interrogated, and many were held in war relocation and military detention centers.

These Americans were suspected of remaining loyal to their ancestral land. Unfortunately, this suspicion was shared by most other non-Japanese-Americans—and this general distrust resonated throughout the United States until after the Cold War.

We all know that painful experiences sometimes trigger the mind's kicking into survival mode, blocking memories that are difficult to process. This story concerns a remarkable woman and her life's journey, which began shortly after World War II. She has no early childhood memories before age six; she believes this is due to the harsh lifestyle she endured during those early years.

Donna was born in Denver, Colorado, after the war ended, to Japanese-American parents. Her father was drafted into the Army, did boot camp twice because of discrimination he faced at Fort Riley, and then volunteered for the United States in the 442nd Regimental Combat Team in World War II. Regretfully, assumptions were made by most people that her family fought for the Japanese.

Can you imagine how the girl's father and mother must have felt, let alone the daughter? How terrible to be viewed as the enemy and taunted by others who tried to make this good family ashamed of their heritage and their very identities. Donna especially hated going to school on December 7; on that day, the anniversary of the Pearl Harbor bombing, the bullying was at its worst. Her favorite days at school were those featuring show and tell, which gave her the opportunity to show off her father's Army photo album and share about his presence in the U.S. Army—proving they were Americans, too!

This beautiful child was raised by second-generation Japanese-American farmers who were proud descendants of samurai warriors, educators, and land owners. Although the war was officially over, her veteran father was still afraid his family would be viewed by the FBI as a threat, even though the family had discarded everything associated with their Japanese heritage. The FBI seized and never returned their ancestral samurai sword that had been passed down through generations.

To be accepted in this difficult situation, they felt they had to immerse themselves in the American lifestyle and abandon their Japanese language and culture.

Another inequity was that of women's subservience to men, which was American "heritage" of the time that was, at least, comparable to Japanese culture. Fortunately, at an early age, Donna recognized this injustice, especially when her aunt made Donna do the dinner dishes while her brothers got to play!

There were days she was glad to be treated differently than her brothers, especially because of the sometimes harsh punishments they endured. Donna was the baby of the family and the only girl, and she admittedly got away with a great deal—although not so much with her strict grandmother, who felt it was her duty to provide traditional Japanese discipline.

In spite of everything, Donna loved people—and what better way to make new friends than to join the Girl Scouts? Here, she easily made friends with fellow Scouts. As she describes it, the Scout leadership helped put her "mind and energies toward something positive," and she learned that a Girl Scout could "overcome any challenge. There are no limits. She can be anything. She can do anything." The Girl Scouts helped her build a lifetime of skills and confidence.

Eventually, she entered the awkward teenage years. Uncomfortable as those times could be, she loved to have fun with her friends. She vividly recalls one story in particular because it changed the direction of her life and led her to God. Donna somehow persuaded her parents to let her spend Christmas vacation with her boyfriend and his family thousands of miles away from her own parents' watchful eyes. This trip marked a significant time in her life, not only because it was the first time away from her parents, but it was also the time when she lost her innocence while developing a relationship with God!

Upon returning home, Donna began to fear the unthinkable of her one-time action with her boyfriend. And unbeknownst to her parents, she briefly contemplated suicide. In the extreme emotion of the moment, not feeling free to discuss her issues with her parents, Donna began to pray to God for a miracle. She believes God gave her that miracle by quieting her fears about the future. Later, she learned it was a false alarm, but this valuable lesson changed the direction of her life. From that day forward, Donna would take her problems to God and stay in faith when the days were dark and long.

## A SENSE OF PURPOSE

*This is what the Lord says: "Look! An eagle is swooping down, spreading its wings…*
—Jeremiah 48:40 (NIV)

In our younger years, most of us do not recognize that we have a purpose in life, let alone what that purpose is. Perhaps, some of us even wonder why we were born. But our lives are sacred, given to us by God. We must always remember our lives have purpose—and, above all, that "what the Lord giveth, only the Lord can taketh away."

This teenage girl's cry for God's help somehow activated her own heart into believing in miracles, changing her life and generations to come. For you see, that day, she realized she had a purpose and that there was something greater than herself. Her purpose would change thousands of lives, some of whom she would never even meet.

The world is truly blessed that this girl's life was spared by her own hands. After this experience, she began searching for ways to use her past to improve her future. She moved from her small town to Houston to live with her older brother and soon met and fell in love with a sweet-talking guy. They were married in the early 1970s. Her new name was Donna Fujimoto Cole. The Cole family increased by one with the birth of a baby girl, Donna's only child. The marriage only lasted eight years, and, as a single mom, Donna knew she had to make more money to survive.

## A LEAP OF FAITH

Donna began working in a male-dominated industry at the age of 23. Due to her hard work (14-hour days), honesty, and desire for quality, she soon became a vice president and 26 percent owner of Del Rey Chemical, as well as a 3 percent owner of its parent company, Gold King Chemical. Throughout her three years at Del Rey, Donna would live and breathe the chemical business, until she was ready to start her own company at age 27. Can you imagine what a huge leap of faith it took for this single parent to use her $5,000 life savings to start her own chemical business?

Now it was time to come up with a name for her new business. She stayed up all night until narrowing it down to three names: Fuji, Fujimoto, or Cole Chemical. She decided against the first two because it was a time of Japanese bashing in the industry, so Cole Chemical was it! Donna's commitment to her daughter's future made her determined to succeed. Clients she dealt with while working for Gold King Chemical—like Shell, DuPont, Monsanto, and Exxon—helped Donna start her own business. Over the next three decades, Donna made a serious commitment to growth by putting assets in the ground and growing the business. She also committed to hiring minorities and women and giving back to the community.

Fast-forward more than 30 years later: Cole Chemical and Distributing, Inc., under the leadership of Donna Cole, provides chemical ingredients to petrochemical manufacturers, oil companies, and personal care product makers. The corporation offers chemicals with supply chain management, custom blending, warehousing, logistics, and custom packaging services from its locations throughout the United States. The company also provides chemical imports and exports.

Like most businesses, Cole Chemical has experienced challenges throughout its 34 years in business. Donna recalls the time her company had to recuperate from the loss of a large, 15-year contract, even though Cole Chemical had won many exceptional quality and service awards. This contract represented 25 percent of the company's profits, and with the loss of revenue, Donna had to lay off people within the company. She reports that it was one of the hardest business decisions she ever had to make. Cole Chemical survived this and other challenges. Today, Donna and Cole Chemical have multiple clients in all 50 states, with a growing international business and annual sales near $100 million.

## DONNA'S THOUGHTS ON SUCCESS

*We only live once, but once is enough if we do it right. Live your life with class, dignity, and style so that an exclamation, rather than a question mark signifies it!*
—Gary Ryan Blair

Donna summarizes her thoughts on and principles of success in a few brief statements:

- Do not let one company or one industry dominate your business.
- Know your industry and business.
- Treat people the way they want to be treated, not how you want to be treated.
- Don't overpromise, but do over deliver.
- Be responsive and positive.
- Give and ask for nothing in return, and good things will happen.
- Be forthright and honest in all dealings.
- Be the best you can be all the time.
- Follow through and up.
- Be persistent.

## Write Your Goals for Success

_____

_____

_____

_____

_____

(Go to www.GodGaveUsWings.com for a free worksheet.)

## PAY IT FORWARD

*We are not here merely to make a living. We are here to enrich the world with a finer spirit of hope and achievement—and we impoverish ourselves if we forget the errand.*
—Woodrow Wilson

At an early age, Donna Cole learned about giving from her generous mother, who would deliver canned goods to the less fortunate during the holidays, in spite of the family's own dire financial situation. Donna is known as a woman of many passions; her enthusiasm extends beyond Cole Chemical. "She embodies our goal of servant leadership—a way of leading to better serve others," reflects Harriet Wasserstrum, president of the American Leadership Forum.

Donna is passionate about helping young girls and women succeed. She has donated her time and resources to numerous organizations, such as Asian Women Empowered, the Center for Asian Pacific American Women, the Women's Business Enterprise Alliance, and the Women in Energy Network.

Donna has been a leading force in sponsoring other organizations, such as the Pipeline for Sciences, which works with underprivileged children, and the Women's Home Board, a facility for women to overcome drug addiction, to name just a few. "I am trying to help mentor young women, to help guide their careers and professional lives," Donna says.

Donna truly "walks the talk." Over 10 years ago, she received a call from Anita Carman about a vision God had put in her heart to start a women's ministries program. Donna recalls that Anita wasn't sure how she was going to finance such a ministry. The next thing Donna knew, she had donated a sizable sum to seed the Inspire Women Conference. This was around the same time Donna had learned her company was losing a major account. Nonetheless, instead of worrying about where she would get the money, she turned it over to God, knowing He would exceedingly and abundantly provide all that she needed.

Donna's donation allowed Anita Carman to implement her vision from God for a women's ministry that would go beyond conferences, to provide mentorship, support, and investment in women looking to unlock their God-given potential. Since its founding, Inspire Women has grown to invest millions in scholarships, grants, and support for women of all races and economic backgrounds. Through its Life Purpose Academy, inner circles, citywide events, and, most importantly, the ministry work of the women they invest in around the world, this organization helps women "find their spark" and follow their God-given calling.

Of course, it's entirely possible that if Donna hadn't taken a huge leap of faith, this ministry would not have gotten off the ground, and thus, thousands would not have found their wings. Donna's giving doesn't stop with girls and women. She also has invested considerable resources into the future of many other children. Donna founded the All-Earth Ecobot Challenge, an engineering competition for fifth through eighth graders, and is working on dismantling the cradle-to-prison pipeline with her American Leadership Forum class.

This woman learned early in life that God would go exceedingly and abundantly above and beyond what she thought possible in her life. Donna took the limits off God, believing He would show her the way to fly. She now soars, teaching others the techniques she learned through her belief in miracles.

Donna Cole has served on numerous national and regional councils, including serving on the President's Export Council during the George H. W. Bush administration.

### List a Few Ways You Can Help Others

_____

_____

_____

_____

_____

## BLESSING PRAYER

My prayer for you is that you will always have faith in knowing that God will keep you and protect you in times of trouble. He will clear your path by shining a flood of light upon you, removing all darkness so you may soar in His grace. Amen.

## NEXT CHAPTER

The next nail-biting story will illustrate how one woman's unfortunate choice many years ago drastically altered future generations, until a courageous woman whose hellacious childhood made her determined to stop the decades of poverty, abuse, and teen pregnancy inherited from previous family's members.

## CHAPTER 7

# Revelation Awaits

*I consider that our present sufferings are not worth comparing with
the glory that will be revealed in us. For the creation waits in eager
expectation for the children of God.*
—Romans 8:18–19 (NIV)

## CAUSE AND EFFECT

Sometimes, you wonder how one decision can drastically alter life
for generations to come. This chapter illustrates an unfortunate
cause and effect stemming from a real story, many years ago. It
involves a migrant farm girl from Mexico, the country where she gave
birth to four children. This young woman must have felt desperate to
support her children after being abandoned by their father. She chose
to move to America and left her young family behind with her parents,

hoping to find a better life for them all. Sadly, as the months turned to years, she somehow lost touch with what she left behind.

The young woman didn't realize the devastating effect her ill-fated choice would have on future generations (as well as herself): poverty, drug abuse, and sexual abuse, along with three generations of teen pregnancy.

Eventually, she would bear five more children, and surprisingly, those children would experience greater poverty than their four half siblings left behind in Mexico with grandparents. The significant difference between the two groups of children? Education. The four children raised in Mexico remarkably completed their educations and became successful citizens, while the children raised in the United States dropped out of school, primarily due to teen pregnancy.

Fast-forward to the present day, the third generation, a young woman whose hellacious childhood made her determined to stop the decades of family devastation. This brave woman, Latasha, would later come to establish a nonprofit organization, the Lilies and Reeds Society, to help prevent teen pregnancies.

Latasha's father was murdered before she was even born. One day, when she asked what had happened to her father, Latasha's mom said, "she was never meant to happen—she was a mistake." She would hear these hurtful words throughout her childhood.

Latasha's earliest memory, at only two years of age, was living in a drug-infested household in Kansas. Illicit sexual activity was present everywhere. Latasha remembers sitting on strangers' laps while they shot up their drug of choice; chaotic arguing and fighting over who took what or who did what to whom would often ensue.

Her mother's ongoing substance abuse and poor choice of partners caused their lives to progressively spiral out of control. Latasha recalls that when she was five years old, her younger brother's father came home higher than a kite, busting down the door and yelling, "I'm home, and I have donuts!" Her mother hurled a toy truck, hitting him in the head. Blood splattered everywhere as he yelled for a frightened Latasha's help, but her mother screamed, "You'd better not move!" He staggered out the door, leaving Latasha to deal with her out-of-control mother. Unfortunately, such traumatic experiences had begun to be the norm for this little girl.

On a day not unlike many other days, Latasha—only six now—was responsible for taking care of herself and her one-year-old brother. Most days such as this, she cradled him like a doll or pushed him around in the stroller, back and forth inside the house, so he'd stop crying—at least until her mother came home to help with his care. This day was different, however, because Latasha's little brother climbed onto the coffee table, lost his balance, and fell to the floor, breaking his leg. Her mother, who was actually home this time, heard a loud scream and came running to see what happened. Not realizing that her son's leg was broken, she tried just comforting him until he fell asleep. The next morning, the baby's leg was severely swollen, and he cried uncontrollably until Latasha's mother took him to the hospital.

The hospital suspected neglect, which was confirmed after talking to Latasha. Child Protective Services swept in, and both Latasha and her brother were placed in foster homes, where they lived for the next two years. Latasha's first foster home, where she stayed for one year, was a group home comprising a variety of age groups; after everything she'd been through, Latasha would now deal with sexual assault and attempted rape by a teenage boy.

## EARTH ANGELS

*I remain confident of this: I will see the goodness of the Lord in the land of the living.*
—Psalms 27:13 (NIV)

At age seven and united with her little brother once again, Latasha settled in with a new foster family. Dorothy and Edward, the pastor of a local church, gave the children both a stable environment and the love they so deserved. For the first time ever, Latasha, as she says, "felt safe and secure," remembering how her foster mother would brush her hair and help her in a myriad of other motherly ways. There was no yelling or fighting. Dorothy and Edward were her earth angels, and Latasha felt loved, more loved than she ever had felt before.

Dorothy and Edward pushed Latasha to do better and to be better. They showed Latasha many important things, such as what good hygiene looked like. They went to church as a family every Sunday, with Bible study on Wednesdays. Then, one dreadful day, it was all taken away. The day her mother was given back custody of her children, Latasha recalls, was "the worst day of my life."

Now that the children were back home with their mother, some things did change—drugs and needles were replaced by the popping of pills, the pushing of pills, and the buying of pills. And some things did not change—the children were still exposed to inappropriate, even illegal, sex within the household; too often, they had to quickly change residences; and they were still left alone.

In the third grade, Latasha found great solace in school and in swimming. She thought she had hit the jackpot when her mother enrolled her in a magnet school, offering a better education and a swimming program. The school was great, but the swimming instructor not so great—he indecently touched Latasha during swimming lessons. Thankfully, the small family moved away after a few months, and Latasha transferred to another school. Like so many abused children, she never told a soul about her previous ongoing molestation.

Thank God for the positive impact of Latasha's fifth-grade teacher, a woman who spent countless hours with her students, using motivational techniques such as class ice cream parties. Her encouraging efforts to teach students everything from math to the states and their capitals (the latter through the use of catchy tunes, something especially useful to Latasha) paid off: Latasha loved her teacher, and she loved school. The school was her refuge, her stable environment. She excelled there, hanging out in the hallways and classrooms as long as she could before being forced to go home.

As Latasha grew into a preteen, she lost all respect for her mother and became very rebellious. At one point, she ran away, but her mother soon found her wandering the streets with nowhere to go, and she ended up back home. Finally, a lucky break occurred: Latasha was sent to live with her 19-year-old sister, who resided with her husband in Oklahoma. Once again, Latasha exchanged her intolerable life for one much more normal—among other things, a weekly family night at home and another blessing of a teacher who regularly instructed her to "lose the excuses if you want to make something of yourself."

Latasha was happy and felt good about her new life…that is, until six months later, when her mother also decided to move to Oklahoma. In less than one year, Latasha's life went from bad to good to worse to horrible, all stemming from her mother's out-of-control life that had included teen pregnancy, drug addiction, lack of education, and poverty. As you may recall from this chapter's beginning, her grandmother's life choices had drastically affected the generations that followed.

## BELIEVE

*Blessed are those who can find light in dark places, courageous enough to feel when it's time to reflect and hopeful enough to believe when all seems impossible…*
—Nikki Rowe

Through no choice of her own, Latasha was living with her mother again. She felt total despair—how would she ever escape her mother's poor choices? The family moved into the bad area of town. Latasha experienced daily bullying from other black girls; they said she didn't look black and used crude language when referring to her facial features. The situation was unbearable. At age 12, Latasha began to black out during fights; onlookers said she would "just go crazy." Once, Latasha recalls, her mother told the police that "I pulled a knife on her and tried to kill her." This resulted in an immediate intervention in which mental health counselors "performed biweekly home visits to see me," says Latasha. "I told them I wasn't crazy; you need to check out my mother, but no one ever listened."

Latasha entered her teenage years. She had her first boyfriend at 10 years of age, but she did not have her first sexual experience until age 13. Shortly after, she met her future son's father at one of the many parties her mom allowed her to attend. On date night, the two would go out with his mother in tow. Latasha loved her boyfriend's mother because she would spend time just with her, taking her to venues such as her own violin performances.

Even after Latasha's mother married and the family moved, the two teenagers continued to date until Latasha was 15 and a sophomore in high school. The pair broke up just before learning Latasha was with child.

It would take until after her baby was born before Latasha would find the courage to break the generational curse. Until then, she continued to live with her mother and stepfather, a hard-drinking preacher who loved to criticize others. Her parents fought constantly, and the preacher's negativity caused Latasha to have no respect for Christianity. At one point, the scenario reached far beyond simple negativity: in

Latasha's eighth month of pregnancy, her stepfather grabbed her by the throat, pinning her up against a wall and choking her nearly into unconsciousness, for "interrupting" her mother and him.

## LIFE-CHANGING

*I lift up my eyes to the mountains—where does my help come from?*
*My help comes from the LORD, the Maker of heaven and earth.*
—Psalms 121:1–2 (NIV)

So, now what? Latasha represented her family's third generation to experience teen pregnancy. Would she drop out of school like the previous generations, or would she enroll in a special school program? She chose to stay in school, attending a secondary high school and enrolling in the Emerson Teen Parent Program, headed by Dr. Norma Leslie. The program offered a three-pronged approach—high school graduation, family foundational skills, and economic independence—with at-risk teen mothers in mind.

Eventually, along with a handful of other young women in the group, Latasha would speak to various charities and potential contributors about the importance of funding such a program, explaining how such education can change the directions of many lives— lives like hers.

Latasha spoke of how the program had turned her life around, giving her tools for a better life. She was consistently surrounded by the school's support system, a group of trained individuals entirely dedicated to her success and with baby Arynn's best interests in mind. Her mentors in the program would not only visit the 15-year-old mother in the hospital when her baby was born, but also many times afterward, especially as there had been complications at birth (the cord had wrapped around the baby's neck); they later offered support for her son's asthma. At age

16, using her newly learned life skills, a brave Latasha and baby moved out on their own. Times were tough. She recalls that many days her only meal consisted of Doritos.

Latasha had always dreamed of being a lawyer. She managed to graduate seventh in her class, which made her eligible to attend Oklahoma City University. The young mom was awarded a scholarship, at age 17, through Oklahoma's Promise. She instead decided to join the U.S. Navy, with a plan to start off as a legalman and then move up into the Judge Advocate General's Corps after finishing college. Just before leaving for boot camp, however, Latasha went on a stealing spree at a major department store, a learned behavior from her past. Looking for an item to give her recruiting officer, she instead acquired a week's jail time. Since it was her first offense and the judge knew that she was in the Navy's Delayed Entry Program, Latasha was not convicted of a felony, but instead given 60 hours of community service and a two-year deferred sentence.

After completing her community service, Latasha was able to go off to boot camp, leaving her young child with a relative. Some of the other enlistees hated the strict environment so much that they resorted to cutting themselves or even jumping out windows to get discharged. Meanwhile, Latasha's military dream was to be the first woman on a submarine.

Unfortunately, Latasha's life in the military was short-lived due to poor health. Her bones were not strong enough to withstand the strenuous workouts, and she began experiencing numerous shin splints and stress fractures. She spent two months in the U.S. Naval Hospital in a wheelchair and on several medications that doctors hoped would strengthen her brittle bones, which were likely caused by her poor diet as a child.

Eventually released from the service and completely devastated by the discharge, Latasha felt she was a veteran by default, hurt in basic training—now, her spirit was broken as well as her bones. To rub salt in her wounds, Latasha received papers that listed her discharge as neither honorable nor dishonorable, but merely as "other." *Am I not worthy of an honorable discharge?* she thought. Latasha went years believing she was not honorable in the eyes of the Navy. One day, she called the Veterans Administration inquiring about her disability rating and received some surprising news: she was, indeed, listed with an honorable discharge. Now finally, she felt at peace knowing that in the military's eyes, she was a worthy person.

At 19, Latasha once again faced the question of what to do with her life. Her mother had sold her car, and she had nowhere to go but to her sister's. Soon after, she began to date a friend, eventually moving in with him. From this union, a baby girl was born. The year was 2002, and Latasha was 21.

Latasha was so accustomed to men being the abusers that she decided in this relationship, she would beat him to the punch by abusing him first. Her mindset was to be in control of every situation and not let a single man tell her what to do. And so, Latasha became the abuser. After physically, mentally, and verbally abusing her daughter's father, she finally began to see that she really did love him and he had loved her. She wanted to change, to try to work it out. But it was too late. His heart had hardened, and there was no love in his eyes, only disgust.

She knew something was wrong and sensed her boyfriend might be seeing someone else. She found herself threatening to kill him and herself if he didn't cut the affair short. She was 22 years old with two children under the age of seven, and she suddenly realized her life was spiraling out of control, in some ways mirroring the life of her own mother.

This was Latasha's first wake-up call. If her life was to change, she needed to change her situation. Living on her own again, Latasha enrolled in college and also got a job working in the school's administrative office, where she met another guy—this time, a good man who wanted to marry her. But because Latasha's model of a man included abuse, she was not attracted to the kind-hearted fellow, and they broke up. He accepted another job, moved away, and got married shortly afterward. "This is one of my biggest regrets," Latasha says today.

It was 2007, and Latasha had begun praying in earnest for the drama in her life to stop. Someone must have been listening, because a friend gave her a CD of Christian music. Fortuitous events, events of grace, began to follow. Latasha's path was finally about to shift.

After her son's basketball practice at the YMCA, Latasha would talk with the coach's wife, Lisa, about life. In spite of the busyness that surrounded her and her six children, Lisa seemed so happy. Latasha wished she could experience such happiness; Lisa possessed a light, joy, and peace, unlike anything Latasha had witnessed so far in life. Latasha began to tell Lisa how she was looking for a new church, that she needed something different. Lisa told Latasha that their church was small, but she was welcome to come anytime.

On New Year's Eve of 2007, Latasha said a prayer. She asked the Lord to remove the drama, promising to dedicate her life to Him. The first of January was a new day, a new year, and she was determined to stay true to her word. Latasha took up Lisa's offer and visited the church that first Sunday of the year. Lisa was right: the church was small, about 25 people, including kids. And yet, in each one of them, a light shone brightly. All were full of joy and peace greater than any she had seen. Latasha hungered more than ever for the Word. One Sunday in March, a basket was passed among the congregation; it was filled with notes of Scripture, one for each person to take and read. Her verse was from

Matthew 12:48 and, at that moment, Latasha knew the church was her new family.

## WHO ARE YOU?

*Someone told him, "Your mother and brothers are standing outside, wanting to speak to you." He replied to him, "Who is my mother, and who are my brothers?" Pointing to his disciples, he said, "Here are my mother and my brothers. For whoever does the will of my Father in heaven is my brother and sister and mother."*
—Matthew 12:47-50 (NIV)

Latasha loved her new family! There was no drama…no screaming…no hitting each other. All she wanted was to totally immerse herself in this loving new lifestyle. And so, she was baptized in March of 2008 and rededicated her life to Jesus.

Latasha realized that, in her situation, for her to truly change, she must cut some family ties. This meant no more family get-togethers during the holidays, especially not at her mother's house. Latasha's new life was free of drinking, foul language, and, most of all, drama. She began hosting Bible study at her home and only listened to music with a positive or uplifting nature. Little by little, she transitioned from fear to a faith-filled life—changing the future for herself, her children, and generations to come.

Still believing that something was missing from her life, Latasha began volunteering in 2009 with a parenting instructor at Putnam City Academy in Bethany, Oklahoma. She simply wanted to share her story to help other teen moms avoid some of the mistakes that she had made. Latasha remembers thinking, *I don't have anything to give*—until she realized her life experiences had already prepared her for this journey.

## BUSINESS

*God often uses our deepest pain as the launching pad for our greatest calling.*

—Unknown

In 2010, Latasha decided to use her life experiences as a guiding light to promote change in her community. She wanted to start a nonprofit called Lilies (Lovely Incredible Leaders Intelligently Escaping Statistics), to educate girls to prevent teen pregnancy, and knew who could help her: she contacted Dr. Norma Leslie from the Emerson Teen Parent Program, who had helped Latasha in her teenage years.

Seeing the need to include educational programs for both girls and boys, Latasha expanded the organization's name to the Lilies and Reeds (Responsible Edifying Educated Dedicated Souls) Society. The nonprofit promotes change, and change is, accordingly, its mission. One can only imagine how proud Latasha was when her teenage son first volunteered to speak at the Lilies and Reeds Society!

Latasha took another bold step toward change: she began homeschooling her son, who was then in the eighth grade and receiving increasingly poor grades. She recognized the signs from her own life and knew a drastic change was needed if she was to stop the generational effects of poverty and abuse.

Today, Latasha is a beacon of light for hundreds of teens in her community. She and Arynn regularly speak about their vision for positive, fulfilling lifestyles: no matter your background, you are not your past, but rather your future.

Latasha has accomplished more than she could have ever imagined. Today, she is especially excited about her son's future: he has already completed aviation ground school training and after completing high school, he plans to attend Southern Nazarene University to get his degree in business aviation. The sky is the limit for this now-Christian family of three—and all because those many years ago, a few people cared enough to show this child she was not worthless, but rather quite valuable, indeed—worth the price of God's only begotten Son.

Latasha's favorite Bible verse says it all:

*For I am convinced that neither death nor life, neither angels nor demons, neither the present nor the future, nor any powers, neither height nor depth, nor anything else in all creation, will be able to separate us from the love of God that is in Christ Jesus our Lord.*
— Romans 8:38-39 (NIV)

## LATASHA'S THOUGHTS ON SUCCESS

- Implement regular time for family devotions.
- Make a date with your child.
- Take time for yourself.
- Spend quality time with God.
- Have mercy on others.
- There are many seasons in your life, and this one is only a fraction of the total number.
- Have determination.
- Practice obedience.
- Just do it!
- Don't give up.
- Encourage yourself through the use of self-affirmation.
- Believe in yourself by realizing you can do all things through Christ.

Latasha's story is an inspiration to us all. Her kind spirit teaches us that it is possible to forgive those who have hurt you, just as she did with her mother. This special lady exemplifies the meaning of a good Christian. She, like the rest of us, is truly worthy of God's love.

### Write Your Goals for Success

_____

_____

_____

_____

_____

(Go to www.GodGaveUsWings.com for a free worksheet.)

## PAY IT FORWARD

*Joy must be one of the pivots of our life. It is the token of a generous personality. Sometimes it is also a mantle that clothes a life of sacrifice and self-giving. A person who has this gift often reaches high summits. He or she is like sun in a community.*
—Mother Teresa

Through the Lilies and Reeds Society, Latasha has the opportunity to pay it forward by using her life experiences, offering teen programs to empower youth in their communities to make positive life choices that enable them to maximize their potential.

The Lilies and Reeds Society's primary purpose is to lower teen pregnancy statistics by filling students with wisdom through mentoring, volunteer work, and fun-filled activities that will encourage them to mentor other young students.

This Teen Parent Mentoring Program is a social network of adults and community members who care about the youth and are committed to helping teens develop and reach positive academic, career, and personal goals.

Latasha Howell, founder and CEO, now reports that "We are a community dedicated to empowering young families and creating the best possible start for young mothers, young fathers, and their babies."

## DID YOU KNOW?

- The United States has the highest teen pregnancy rate in the industrialized world—twice as high as the United Kingdom or Canada and 10 times greater than Switzerland.
- The U.S. teen birth rate dropped nine percentage points—to the lowest birth rate since 1946—from 2009 to 2010.
- About one in every three U.S. women are pregnant at least once before they turn 20.
- Approximately 750,000 U.S. teens get pregnant each year.
- Oklahoma has the second highest teenage birth rate in the United States for girls aged 15–17 and is number one for girls 18–19.

For more information or to make a donation, go to http://www.liliesandreedssociety.org.

### List a Few Ways You Can Help Others

_____

_____

_____

_____

_____

**BLESSING PRAYER**

May you forgive others like others have forgiven you, and have the wisdom to know that today does not last forever and your future is not based on your past. May your life be guided by faith, believing God will show up when you call His name. Amen.

**NEXT CHAPTER**

The next story will take you on an incredible journey with a young black American girl growing up in Taiwan in the early 1960s, temporarily escaping the pain of discrimination—and later having the thrill of wearing Princess Diana's necklace on her wedding day.

## CHAPTER 8

# The Art of Love

*Your struggle becomes your strength by learning something that will get you to the other side.*

—Deborah Duncan

## WHOSE WINGS?

magine growing up in Taiwan in the early 1960s as an American black girl, temporarily escaping the pain of discrimination—until age 11 and an unsettling move back to the United States. Born in Oklahoma City but moving abroad with her Air Force family at three months of age, Deborah Duncan remembers well those early days in Taiwan: if you were from the United States, you were neither black nor white, you were simply American.

Looking back on those first years in Taiwan—and in Japan—it's no surprise that Deborah ended up in the communications business. Her family was moving from place to place; young Deborah would attend five different elementary schools. At each school, she was determined to learn everything she could about her "new friends," thereby honing her future interviewing skills. She completed school in San Antonio, Texas, where her father retired.

Deborah was raised in a middle-class family by both parents, with two siblings—a six-year-older sister and a three-year-younger brother. Her family of five rarely displayed any affection toward one another; they believed their actions spoke louder than their words.

Her earliest childhood memory, in Taiwan, involved her older sister, who Deborah affectionately called "My Kay." She recalls watching her 11-year-old sister and friends jumping over a sewage ditch every day to play on the other side. Because Deborah was only five, she was too small to master such a feat, preferring instead to sit on the bank for hours and wait for her adored sister to return.

Her big sister finally decided to hand-make Deborah a beautiful pair of cloth wings to fly over the funky-smelly ditch. Little Deborah was so excited because now she would finally get to play with the big kids! In several days' time, the wings were ready: strapped and snug on her back, Deborah headed for the door under the ever-watchful eye of her mother who, surprisingly, asked no questions.

Wings and all, Deborah reached the site in record time. With her sister and friends watching from the other side, she took off running and jumped up into the air...and crashed into the water, facedown into the awful, slimy pit. Climbing from the ditch, covered in muck, one can only imagine how dejected she must have felt, especially with the once-idolized sister's hysterical laughter ringing in her ears.

Anyone growing up with an older sibling knows firsthand about humiliation—and about pranks. So, of course, Deborah was quite familiar with both. This little girl truly wanted to fly, but she needed to wait until her wings developed on their own accord.

## THE CAPACITY OF LOVE

*Words can seal. Words can kindle. Words soothe souls. Words can care. Words love to share. Words express love. Words are alive.*
—Debasish Mridha

Deborah grew up living a good life in a nice house with most of life's amenities. But she rarely experienced any physical signs of affection—nor did she hear the words "I love you." These things were simply not the family norm. One day, Deborah witnessed a friend's mother affectionately say those three important words to her daughter. Standing there in awe of the message (and yet, how foreign it sounded!), she suddenly felt as if a spear had pierced her heart, as she fully realized how much she'd missed hearing those beautiful words from her parents.

Feeling the need, Deborah devised a plan to get her parents to say "I love you" to her. Sounds simple, but this was a big deal for a family who rarely displayed this type of emotion. Deborah had it planned down to the most minute detail: *Okay, I'll take a bath…say goodnight…add a hug and say "I love you"…wait for a response…run off…and go to bed.* Wow, that sounds stressful. And it was for this child. In return for her efforts, she received a resemblance of the words from her shocked parents, but not with the same heartfelt tone she'd heard earlier that day from her young friend's mother. *What is wrong with me?* Deborah wondered. That feeling persisted throughout her life, a longing to hear those words, to feel loved.

## FINDING TRUTH

*Guide me in your truth and teach me, for you are God my Savior,*
*and my hope is in you all day long.*
—Psalm 25:5 (NIV)

Deborah's family would move back to the United States when she was in sixth grade, and she quickly learned about discrimination. No longer called an American but instead often subjected to racial slurs and epithets, she attended a majority white school in San Antonio.

Thankfully, Deborah met her lifelong friend, Catherine, on the first day of school—just after her new friend-to-be was roughed up in the hallway. Disheveled and lost, Catherine walked into the classroom just wanting to go home. "Sit next to me," Deborah told her; after all, she knew how it was to feel alone. Friends to this day, the two girls were blind to their differences and turned out to be each other's biggest cheerleaders, always encouraging one another to reach for the stars.

Deborah recalls that she "really didn't get Black History Month"— that is, until one day in her American history class when she read about an African-American woman named Barbara Jordan. Deborah had finally found a black woman who played a role in the civil rights movement and then integrated into the primarily white male political arena. Barbara Jordan was the first African-American elected to the Texas Senate after Reconstruction, the first Southern black woman elected to the United States House of Representatives, and the first African-American woman to deliver the keynote address at a Democratic National Convention. She received the Presidential Medal of Freedom, among numerous other honors, and was a member of the Peabody Awards Board of Jurors from 1978 to 1980.

Deborah knew she had to meet this Barbara Jordan—but how? Then came one of those weird bits of serendipity that might make the whole thing possible—her school was taking a selected group on a summer field trip to Washington, DC, to visit the White House. Could this be her chance to meet the larger-than-life woman?

Catherine saw the fire in Deborah's eyes surrounding the remote chance of meeting Jordan. "You just have to ask your mom if you can go!" Catherine urged her. The biggest hurdle, of course, was the cost of the privately funded trip: $375. That was a lot of money for a middle-class family in the 1970s, when an average weekly salary was perhaps $175.

As Deborah expected, the answer was "no." However, this did not deter Catherine from talking Deborah into writing Barbara Jordan a letter to solicit her help in getting Deborah's mother to say "yes." So Deborah wrote, then checked the mail daily for a response. A few weeks later, she received her long-awaited letter. "Dear Mrs. Duncan," Barbara Jordan wrote, "education must be your first concern—if it's in any way possible to send your daughter, I will meet her on the steps of Congress."

Taking the letter to heart, the Duncans borrowed the money to send their child on the junior high school trip. And true to her word, Barbara Jordan was waiting on the steps of Congress to greet the 30 delegates from San Antonio, Texas—especially the only black girl in the entire school, the one who took the initiative to write her a letter. The meeting between Deborah Duncan and Barbara Jordan confirmed the lesson that had been slowly formulating in Deborah's mind: Look…look…we are the same, and we can accomplish big things, no matter our color.

Now, the bright-eyed girl entered John Marshall High School, a school struggling at the time with integration. And once again, she endured racial slurs for her "different" looks. But being different can be good, as Deborah notes: "Different gives you a chance to be noticed, because people are paying attention."

Deborah was in drama and was a band geek who played the flute throughout high school. She recalls that, out of the blue, Catherine blurted out at lunch, "You're going to be our homecoming queen one day." Deborah started laughing. "Where did that come from?" she snorted at Catherine, who replied, "I just know it." "Well, Catherine," retorted Deborah, "I guess you haven't noticed what these kids have been calling me!"

And then, senior year, the unimaginable happened: Deborah was listed in the queen's court top 6. She thought it was a prank. *Why are they playing such a mean joke?* She thought, followed by, *What if...*and then acceptance, followed by a real shift in thinking. *They don't understand,* she mused. *I am not who they think I am; why are they doing this?* And then she noticed her little brother in the hallway sporting a poster that said VOTE FOR MY SISTER. Yep, it was real!

Deborah was in the field for band practice when the band director told everyone to "vote for our girl." Deborah's father was in the field with her, waiting to hear the results, when it came time to reveal the new homecoming queen. And then she heard the announcement: "Deborah Duncan is the school's next homecoming queen!"

In addition to Deborah, quite a few other people were shocked (especially the head cheerleader). Some even got vocal, but the majority were happy; they said Deborah was always kind to everyone. Deborah's self-confidence soared, but it also left her with a sense of responsibility to earn everyone's respect, to pay back this debt.

## DREAM TO FLY!

*You become excellent when you fly at a level that creates a wide gap between where you were before and where you are now. Fly like the eagle; the eagle flies as if it never remembered it was once an egg!*
—Israelmore Ayivor

Deborah went on to attend the University of Texas at Austin, earning a degree in radio, television, and film. After graduating, she worked a couple of years in radio, making the switch to television as a reporter for the CBS station in Austin. She remembers living paycheck to paycheck early in her career; of necessity, she became quite ingenious with her limited budget.

In the 1980s, Deborah recalls, one could buy different pieces of Units clothing and create an entire wardrobe from them. *Wow, what a great idea*, Deborah thought, promptly purchasing a knit skirt, shirt, belt, and leggings, all in black. Each day, to change up the look a bit, she would sew, for instance, yellow rickrack on her collar to anchor the morning news, and at night, she would wash the item, then remove the yellow trim and replace it with blue rickrack for the next day's show. On festive occasions, such as for the company's Christmas party, she took it up a notch and added black rhinestones.

All was well until Deborah overheard two women gossiping about her in the editing booth. "Can you believe she wears the same outfit every day?" exclaimed one, to which the other replied, "Oh, my god! It's so embarrassing!" "You know she says she walks to work for the exercise, but it's because she doesn't even own a car!" "Oh, my god!"

The next thing she knew, Deborah rushed into the room, yelling, "Look, I am doing the best I can! I am all alone; you all have husbands! I am doing the best I can!" and then, impulsively, she said, "One day, I am going to have a Rolex and a BMW!" She ran out, thinking, *But what does that even mean?*

Deborah's sudden outburst set the ball in motion for her. One day, she would get that Rolex and BMW. (*See, I told you so!* she thought), later realizing these were actually for validation, but, at least, she got to wear the finest watch in the world (and could always sell it, if desired, for profit!).

Now, Deborah was really on her way. She got a new job as the anchor at the local ABC station, later moving to Dallas, where she started a talk show called *Good Morning Texas* at WFAA-TV, the sister station of KHOU-TV. Deborah and her show's co-host were asked to anchor the morning news there.

After three years, now 34, Deborah decided to move to New York to co-host a talk show for Lifetime Television called *Our Home*. She was at the top of her game—her own personal driver, a move to the Upper East Side, and more money than she'd ever imagined possible—that is, until she almost died.

## A CHANGE IN DIRECTION

*Show me your ways, Lord, teach me your paths.*
—Psalm 25:4 (NIV)

It should have been a morning like any other, but that day Deborah awoke feeling like someone had sliced through her head with an ax. "I couldn't call it a headache," she remembers. "I knew it was something else. I knew something was really, really wrong."

Through the excruciating pain, her thoughts ran wild. She knew this couldn't be just a migraine; it wasn't spinal meningitis or a host of other options (her alternate career choice had been a neurosurgeon). It had to be a broken blood vessel. Pins and needles prickled one side of her body; the other half went numb. *I'm dying*, she thought. *I'm going to die.* She didn't know if she should call her mother to say goodbye: *I will never get a word in, and I'll die on the phone.* She didn't want to hit a New York City emergency room without a gaping wound. She recalled, however, that one of her guests on the show that day was a physician, so she pulled herself together as best she could and hurried off to work. The guest doctor said it was just a headache. Deborah told him she didn't get headaches.

She taped the first segment despite the pain, looking at the 70 people on the set and thinking, *I can't leave; if I do, I'll put them out of work.* When lunch hour arrived, Deborah arrived at a plan: she would go to the hospital, get an MRI, come back, tape the rest of the show, and have surgery that night.

Things didn't go exactly as planned. The pain was now unbearable. Deborah asked her assistant to drive her to the hospital and to be a spokesperson in case she blacked out, or worse. Off they went to New York Cornell Hospital's emergency room, where they sat waiting for what seemed forever. In sheer desperation, the assistant finally screamed, "My boss has an aneurysm, and she is going to die if she doesn't get medical attention!" That got a nurse to come out and ask what was going on. Deborah told her she needed an MRI, and the nurse said, "That's an expensive test." Deborah assured her she had plenty of insurance and a checkbook in her purse—then promptly passed out.

She woke up in the ICU hallway because no beds were available. She remembers the doctor telling her, yes, she had an aneurysm, and too much blood was present in her brain to operate; they needed to wait until the blood dried up so he could locate the ruptured vessel. In some way, Deborah felt lucky; the location of the aneurysm bought them time to run much-needed tests before surgery. Deborah remembers the doctor saying, "We've given you some medication to slow down the bleeding, and we will need to go cap this thing off." And then he gave her a one-in-ten chance of survival.

Through the haze, Deborah heard another voice in the background: "Why is there a patient in the hallway?" It just happened to be Paul McClure, the news director with WMBC. Of course, this is all it took—people started to find out that Deborah Duncan, the talk show host, was in the hospital. Friends from Dallas began calling friends in New York to check on her. In that first week, Ross Perot sent her flowers and called the station, both former Presidents George W. Bush (then governor of Texas) sent a letter telling Deborah that he and Laura were praying for her, and former President George H. W. Bush sent a letter to the hospital as well. The support from Texas was heartening, to say the least.

Imagine what the hospital personnel was thinking. *Who is this woman, that a billionaire, a governor, and a former president of the United States all expressed concern over her care?* The hospital most likely was no longer concerned about the pricey MRI. And even though they still weren't sure exactly who this Texas girl was, you can bet the hospital didn't want her to die on their watch!

The news about Deborah took off like a freight train. Churches began holding prayer services, radio stations had "Deborah watch," and the *New York Times* reported on her stay. Friends she hadn't seen in years began showing up at the hospital. One memorable visit occurred when Leonard Steinberg, the fashion designer, walked more than 10 blocks with a gallon of half-melted ice cream to give to his beloved friend, whom he had previously met in Dallas when he designed her clothes.

Joey Vallone and family, of the famous Vallone restaurants in Houston, used their contacts in New York to cater in food for the neurology department's doctors and nurses so that they would take good care of Deborah. She remembers an intern thanking her over and over again because, as a new doctor, he couldn't afford this type of food. "At the time," says Deborah, "I didn't even know what he was talking about, and I wondered what I might have said or done in my sleep." Everyone was helping in any possible way they knew.

The night before surgery, the surgeon discussed with Deborah the surgical risks: a 30 percent chance she would die while in surgery, a 30 percent chance of an outcome resulting in limited motor skills, a 30 percent chance of coma, and only a 10 percent chance of full recovery. He asked if she needed anything to sleep and if she wanted to pray with him. The odds weren't stacked in her favor. So, she handed it over to God.

## FINDING FAITH

*Fear imprisons, faith liberates; fear paralyzes, faith empowers; fear disheartens, faith encourages; fear sickens, faith heals; fear makes useless, faith makes serviceable.*
        —Harry Emerson Fosdick

Once Deborah surrendered, all her fears evaporated. She asked God to take control of the scalpel and the surgeon's hands. And she accepted: "I was okay either way. If I died, I would get to see my brother who passed away earlier in my life at the hands of a drunk driver, but if I lived, I had more to do."

What followed was a revelation. Deborah had always known she wanted to do something big, maybe even on the order of Mother Teresa. But she suddenly realized that you can't do anything big if you do nothing. Because Deborah had only wanted to make a big difference, she had been paralyzed into doing nothing...or so she thought.

Thoughts began going through her head. *What if I die right now? God, I haven't done all of the things I wanted to do.* She started beating herself up: *What a loser!...I may never get a second chance, and then, but what if I do get a second chance? What will I do differently?* She lay weeping her heart out, apologizing over and over for all she believed she hadn't done.

Deborah heard a knock on the door. It was the nurse, delivering several large bags filled with letters from her viewers. At that moment, another epiphany occurred: you can't put things off—just do it! The letters made her feel loved, and two in particular truly touched her heart.

One, a big envelope from the children's hospital in Dallas, Texas, read something like this:

*Dear Ms. Duncan,*

*We are all praying for you, and we all know you had an aneurysm (a vein that bleeds in your head). We want to thank you for making us laugh even when we don't feel like laughing. We saw on the news you were in the hospital and wanted to send you this squirt gun to use when the doctors bug you…and they will. When you can't take it anymore—you can squirt them so they will go away!*

The second letter was from a lady who said Deborah had saved her life:

*Dear Deborah,*

*One day after my husband had left me, I was going to commit suicide by shooting myself but couldn't decide if it should be in my head or heart. I pulled the gun from the nightstand and laid it on my chest, agonizing over whether it should be my head or chest over and over—then I heard loud laughter coming from my living room TV, and it piqued my curiosity enough that I got up to check it out. There you were, acting like you were trying out for the Dallas Cheerleaders. I began to laugh! I realized at that moment, if I was laughing, I was still alive. I took control of my circumstances and got help, and I am now being treated for depression. Thank you for saving my life!*

The serendipity of the two letters? Deborah had read them right before going into surgery. She believes it was her validation from God that she had, in fact, made a difference in the lives of others.

> *God showed me what people would say about me at my funeral while I was still alive.*
> —Deborah Duncan

The lesson Deborah learned was to get out of God's way and to let Him do His will through her. He will use you in the way He has chosen for you, and you don't have to figure it out. Just be in the moment. Today, Deborah lives by these words: "I am here…I am open…and I am intuitive."

Deborah survived the four-hour surgery, accomplished full recovery, and was back at work in less than a month.

## A MOMENT'S NOTICE

> *With your own wish and desires, never accept alternative offered chances, only stand strong, to making your own choice into reality. You will stand a chance to be what you wish to be with your own words.*
> —Auliq Ice

Her one-year contract was almost up when Deborah got a call at work one morning from Walter Liss, chairman of Buena Vista Television, a division of ABC Disney. Walter asked if Deborah could make a 3:00 p.m. meeting with him and his bosses in Los Angeles. Deborah didn't have much leeway since the flight time was 5 hours and 45 minutes, but with a "no problem, I'll be there" response, she grabbed some clothes from the wardrobe department and headed to the airport.

Here lies the problem: the outfits Deborah hurriedly took were all size 2, and she wore a size 6 at the time. Deborah had to improvise and did what any girl would have done—she squeezed herself into a size 2 and told herself she would be fine if she only took shallow breaths.

Size 2 and all, she made the 3:00 o'clock meeting in Los Angeles and listened with great interest while ABC executives expressed their concerns that Oprah might not re-sign her show's contract. Deborah had met Oprah on several occasions, first interviewing her in the 1980s, and she would do so again on several other occasions, including after Hurricanes Katrina and Ike, and when Deborah hosted her daytime talk show. At any rate, the ABC executives wanted to put *The Debra Duncan Show* into production by 1998, with plans to syndicate it if Oprah did not sign. Deborah agreed, saying, "I had no thought that she would quit back then [and she didn't], but it was exciting to do such a fun show, just in case."

Deborah signed a four-year contract with ABC Disney to host *The Debra Duncan Show*. With some additional negotiations, the parties agreed to run the program out of Houston, where Deborah would be closer to her aging parents, who lived in San Antonio. After finishing her contract with ABC, Deborah performed several interviews and pilots "because they were fun," but, in the end, decided it was time to return to her roots in the business—news. She had other opportunities offering more money and bigger platforms but wisely realized that her work choices affected her entire life, and her life was in Texas.

So, in December 2002, Deborah joined KHOU-TV, Channel 11, as an anchor on *KHOU 11 News This Morning*. And after six years at that news desk, she returned to the talk show format, this time as host of *Great Day Houston*. The show, produced locally by KHOU-TV, airs daily during the week and boasts many thousands of viewers.

## ENDINGS BECOME BEGINNINGS

*He has made everything beautiful in its time. He has also set eternity in the human heart; yet no one can fathom what God has done from beginning to end.*
—Ecclesiastes 3:11 (NIV)

Later, Deborah went through a bout of depression. *Why am I depressed?* she wondered. *I have a great job, money, and a fancy house.* After all was said and done, though, she didn't feel loved. She felt as if she were merely a robot. At one point, she contemplated ending it all to stop the pain.

Through the encouragement of friends, Deborah began seeing a therapist who helped her work through the cause of her depression. She realized that among all of the stuff from her childhood, once thought to be insignificant, there was a vital missing piece. Deborah didn't endure abuse like some, but what she did endure was the absence of those precious words a child longs to hear: "I love you."

After just three sessions, she came to the conclusion that everyone shows love differently and that her parents were no exception. They showed their love to their children by giving them shelter, clothing them, and taking care of them when they were sick. Deborah's parents knew no other way; this behavior had been carried forward for generations. She also realized that her style of love included spoken words, words that she so desperately missed hearing as a child.

Such realizations made Deborah feel better about herself, and the depression began to subside gradually. She also realized she didn't need to have a significant other in her life to be happy.

She stopped by one day to speak with her therapist about being on her show, and while waiting in the reception area, a man showed up. He took one look at Deborah, and said, "Well, I guess our doctor double-booked us; tell her Neal came by," and abruptly left. Little did Deborah know that the brief encounter would change her life forever.

The therapist, Marsha, came out and asked Deborah if a guy had dropped by, for she had asked both Deborah and the other fellow to come at the same time. "Yes, there was a guy, and he seemed upset," replied Deborah. "What did you think of him?" Marsha asked. "I think the two of you are compatible—you should go out." Deborah was less than enthusiastic: "But he's a white guy, and I've never dated outside my race." Marsha raised her eyebrows in a hopeful sort of manner. "Okay," sighed Deborah. "Maybe."

Marsha called Neal but had to leave a message, as it turned out he was attending a wedding in England. He did, however, call Deborah upon his return.

"It sounds like Marsha seems to think we should go out," Neal said.

Deborah kiddingly replied, "Maybe, but my concern is the day we met, you seemed a little frigid, and you could be a serial killer, but I can't ask Marsha because of the confidentiality thing."

"Neal said, jokingly, Marsha does relationships. I go to someone else for my serial killing problem. The good news is, I haven't killed in a while—so do you want to have dinner tonight?"

"Sounds great!"

They went out and had a great time and many more, for over a year. One of Marsha's mantras was that after a year of dating, you should state your intentions. You don't have to get married; you just need to know you are both on the same page and whether or not you should call it quits.

So, after one year, Deborah gave Neal a date by which she wanted to get married, and, in typical businessman style, Neal asked for an extension. She gave him a one-month extension and no more ("I'm not as nice as the IRS"); one month later at dinner, on June 24, Deborah prepared herself for the popping of the question. But none came. Not one word.

Deborah left and went home. Neal woke up in terror, realizing he may have just messed up big time. He knew he had to show up with a ring, and the only place open at 8:00 a.m. was a nearby grocery store, Fiesta, that had a jeweler's cart. Luckily, the jeweler kept early hours, and Neal was able to purchase a ring and hightail it over to Deborah's house. Neal professed his love with, "My life would fall apart without you . . . will you marry me?" Deborah was too smitten to say anything but "yes!"

Now, it was time to make it all official. The Fiesta ring ended up making its way to a famous jeweler for enhancement, and Houston-based London designer Vanessa Riley created a one-of-a-kind wedding dress ensemble for the bride. Deborah decided to follow the typical wedding tradition of "something old, something new, something borrowed, and something blue." The "borrowed" part was really spectacular: Jim McIngvale, a good friend of Deborah's who had built the most lucrative furniture stores in the country, offered to lend her jewelry he had bought at auction: a Princess Diana necklace and earrings set worth over $700,000, which of course came complete with an armed security guard.

On October 27, arm in arm with her proud papa, Deborah Kay Duncan—Houston's award-winning talk show hostess and one beautiful bride—walked down the aisle and into the arms of her husband-to-be, George Neal Horner.

## LIFE TRANSFORMATIONS

Three years later, Deborah and Neal were blessed with a handsome baby boy, Duncan, after her maiden name. "Loosely translated," Deborah says, "his name means 'brown warrior,' which he is." Deborah loves

Duncan in the way she always wanted to be loved, showering her son with warm affection and loving words of praise. His parents have now been married for over 14 years. Duncan is a teenager who still likes to hang out with his cool mom; he thinks that her "public personality" just means she has a lot of friends.

Deborah Duncan is truly a remarkable woman, enchanting everyone she meets with her charisma and beautiful smile. Her story demonstrates, among other things, that everyone has a different capacity to show love. And like everything surrounding us, we need balance in our lives. Sometimes those three little heartfelt words are essential to feeling loved.

## DEBORAH'S THOUGHTS ON SUCCESS

Deborah believes that by setting goals, you may pass up better things that come along. For this reason, she does not set goals but is instead open to whatever comes her way—and she prays for discernment. Deborah is very appreciative of all she has received in this life: "I know God has given me much more than what I would have ever given myself. I still don't think I am deserving."

- Get out of your own way.
- Be quiet enough to hear your inner thoughts.
- Don't underestimate the value of *you*.
- Ask for what you want.
- Find a relationship that is going to enhance your life.
- Love with an undemanding heart.
- Love, give, and do without expecting anything in return.
- Look at everyone and every situation with a third eye.
- Live the life you have until you get the one you want.
- Put blinders on, and go where you want to go.

Deborah Duncan is the recipient of many local and national awards, including five Emmys, two Gracie Allen Awards, and a Telly Award. She continues as the talk show hostess on *Great Day Houston*, which airs on KHOU-TV.

### Write Your Goals for Success

_____

_____

_____

_____

_____

(Go to www.GodGaveUsWings.com for a free worksheet.)

## PAY IT FORWARD

*None of us can single-handedly save the world, but all of us together can certainly make it better.*
—Deborah Duncan

Deborah's achievements on the air are transcended by her commitment and dedication to community service. She is passionate about many causes and chairs numerous community events. She serves on the national board of directors for Mothers Against Drunk Drivers and is a board member for the Palmer Drug Abuse Program. She also volunteers as the emcee for many charitable events to help local charities. Deborah has a beautiful voice, and she loves to use her talent to help others.

### *List a Few Ways You Can Help Others*

_____

_____

_____

_____

_____

Hopefully, you can see that life is more about how you maneuver through challenges from A to Z (but not always in that order). All of us have hurdles in life to overcome, but remember, you have the free will to choose: climb over…go around…bust through…or give up. It's ultimately up to you…either crawl or fly!

## BLESSING PRAYER

My prayer is that you will always feel God's infinite love throughout your life. May you truly enjoy the abundant life He has in store for you, and may you live—and thrive in—a life that is filled with peace and favor. Amen.

## NEXT CHAPTER

The next chapter is a beautiful story filled with love about a first-generation Italian-American girl, who would later grow up to marry into restaurant royalty. She would later discover a startlingly secret saving her life and possibly thousands of others.

## CHAPTER 9

# Blessings Abound

*May the God of Hope fill you with all joy and peace, as you trust in him so that you may overflow with hope by the power of the Holy Spirit.*

—Romans 15:13 (NIV)

### CHANGING LIVES

Four words every woman dreads to hear: "I am so sorry…" Now, imagine hearing those awful words followed by "you've got breast cancer." At first, your heart stops beating, and then your mind begins to run out of control, believing the worst will happen.

Donna Grace Vallone's story, in the beginning, was no different—she, like so many other women diagnosed with breast cancer, was terrified at the mere mention of the words. Her story ultimately takes a turn with her ongoing and persistent mission to save lives. As one who was fortunate to hail from an Italian-American family with the financial resources to afford the country's best doctors and hospitals, Donna chose to pay it forward.

Just like every other breast cancer patient who hears those shocking and scary words for the first time, Donna expected the worst. It wasn't long, however, before her darkest hours morphed into a realization that the early diagnosis, was a lucky one. Sadly, unlike those of several other family members—and hundreds of women worldwide who lose their lives every day from this horrific disease.

Donna learned that approximately 12 percent of women in the general population develop breast cancer at some point in their lives. Moreover, according to the most recent estimates, 55–65 percent of women inheriting the harmful BRCA1 genetic mutation and around 45 percent of women inheriting the BRCA2 mutation will develop breast cancer by the age of 70.

However, Donna also learned that if detected early enough, breast cancer patients now have a five-year survival rate of 100 percent. She soon realized that a diagnosis of breast cancer is not an automatic death sentence.

Donna, thus knew that because of early detection, she was given the gift of life; she became determined to ensure that her daughters and others received that same gift. The story that follows not only focuses on Donna's recovery but also celebrates an ongoing full and happy life—and tells of a life experience and influence that continues to help save lives today (including her own!) and hopefully for generations to come.

## SEEING STARS

*For my part, I know nothing with any certainty, but the sight of the stars makes me dream.*

—Vincent van Gogh

Donna is first-generation Italian-American. She was born in Olympia, Washington, and at three months of age was transplanted to Houston, where she later attended Holy Name Elementary. Donna fondly remembers her grandparents, who lived a few houses down the street: "They always made me feel special and, most of all, loved." Donna realizes how fortunate she was to grow up in such a close-knit Italian-American family.

The oldest of 21 grandchildren, Donna cherished every chance she had to spend time at the home of her "second parents." "My grandmother, Antoinette Chiavone Danna, came to America from Italy when she was just 13 years old," says Donna, "and she always made me feel like I was the best thing in the world. I was never insecure because my grandparents' love gave me the power to believe I was capable of all things." What a powerful gift to give a child!

Donna's heart sang every time she saw her second parents. "I saw stars at the very sight of my grandfather," she says. One can only imagine how difficult it must have been for the young girl to witness her loving grandfather's stroke when he was only 58 years of age. Like most stroke victims, her hero was in a very fragile state. Not to worry, said her grandmother bravely; she would rig the house with all sorts of things to help strengthen her husband. She even strategically placed a magic slate with words written on it to help him speak again. No matter what she did, however, he would never fully recover. He passed away only three years later, at the age of 61.

## LIFE MEMORIES

*The Time and Energy we invest in others, people will take it and carry it with them.*
                                        —Ken Poirot

Today, we know that teachers are to inspire our children, not to crush their gentle spirits, but this wasn't always the case for Donna in grade school. Lingering memories left her crying for days—one, in particular, involved the cruel behavior of a disciplinarian nun (Donna attended Catholic school through high school). Donna recalls the teacher ridiculing her in front of the class about leaving early to go to a rodeo with her family. Thankfully, not all people (or nuns) are alike. There was Sister Stanislaus, for instance, a fun-loving nun in Donna's high school who even wore makeup along with her traditional religious habit and who would act out Shakespeare every chance she got.

Donna's biggest challenge back then concerned the stigma attached to being overweight. Sadly, she endured ongoing teasing from the boys in her class. Out of love, her mother put Donna on a diet and began delivering healthy lunch alternatives to school. For a while, nothing seemed to help, but then Donna entered high school and started liking boys, and that's all it took for her to begin shedding the pounds.

When she was growing up, Donna and her family (which included two siblings: a brother and a sister) attended Holy Name Church on the north side of Houston. Her father was very involved in church and believed volunteering was a good way to give back—and whatever Dad did, Donna did; that included not only various volunteer opportunities, but also singing in the church choir. One of Donna's fondest childhood memories was staying up late with her beloved father to watch television, which included Friday night wrestling matches (she knew all the wrestlers' names by heart). It was not necessarily something the rest of the family enjoyed, but it gave Donna and her dad quality time together. Donna says her father was "a brilliant man and initially wanted to be a doctor; however, his father died while he was in high school, forcing him to work to help support his mother." Nevertheless, her dad instilled in Donna a love of education and the importance of getting a college degree, though this was not typical for women of her era, especially in Houston's Italian community.

Donna loved school and ranked number one in her eighth-grade class; she graduated from high school 16th in a class of 174 and was one of the few girls to attend college. In the meantime, the community had noticed her beauty, and the Houston Press named Donna, a top-five finalist in the Miss Teenage Houston competition.

*Rather, it should be that of your inner self, the unfading beauty*
*of a gentle and quiet spirit, which is of great worth in God's sight.*
—1 Peter 3:4 (NIV)

Donna earned a bachelor's degree in music education from the University of Houston, where she made the dean's list. This humble woman who appreciates her loving family and the values they've inspired in her says she is "glad my dad raised the bar for me to strive to do better than other women of the time. My father would say, 'Women who don't have morals like yours…make it harder for women who have morals like yours.'"

After college, Donna taught music for 14 years in the Houston Independent School District at various elementary and middle schools. Then, abruptly, at the early age of 36, she became a widow with young children. This was a stressful time for her, but she remained grounded by working every day, doing what she loved most, outside of her family: teaching music at Houston's T. H. Rogers School. This is a Vanguard school entirely devoted to teaching special needs and gifted children from across the entire district. The school has a specialized staff of over 200 who address the learning requirements and individual needs of the very diverse student population. This school serves more than 100 multiply impaired students, from the deaf to those enrolled in the K–8 Vanguard Magnet program, striving for the ultimate goal of making each student a well-rounded individual able to reach his or her full potential in the world. As you might imagine, these beautiful children gave Donna what she needed most at a challenging time—lots of hugs and love, the essential meaning of life.

> *Start children off on the way they should go, and even when they are old they will not turn from it.*
> —Proverbs 22:6 (NIV)

Within a year, Donna was in charge of music for the upcoming Italian Festival. Her uncle suggested she contact Tony Vallone, the owner of Tony's, a respected local restaurant, to get in touch with free-of-charge opera singers for the program. It took several calls, but Tony finally agreed to meet with her to discuss the music. During the conversation, it emerged that they were both in need of a walking buddy, and the two decided to meet after work to stroll together. Tony had been a single dad for five years at that point, and he soon became an excellent resource for Donna in her new role as a single mother. She began looking forward to her walks with Tony. Donna said, "Tony became my best friend, showing me such compassion and kindness." She was falling head over heels for this gentle giant. "I knew the first time we met that I wanted him in my life." For his part, Tony says that he knew Donna was the marrying kind but wasn't sure if he was ready to get married again. Even so, little by little, the two began to fall in love with their soulmates.

Donna and Tony found themselves invited to the same wedding. As Tony was about to leave after the wedding, just before the reception,

Donna joked, "Surely you're not going to leave the merry widow alone at an Italian wedding?" After that, they went out to dinner. Two years later, in 1984, they married, and they have been inseparable ever since.

Life was good for the newlyweds and their blended families. A year later, their joy expanded as they welcomed another child—a daughter—into their family. The following years mostly witnessed the typical ebb and flow of life, but in the midst of those years, Donna and her family began to uncover a family "secret" that would forever change their lives.

## THE GIFT OF LIFE

*Be strong and courageous. Do not be afraid or terrified because of them, for the Lord your God goes with you; he will never leave you nor forsake you.*
—Deuteronomy 31:6 (NIV)

Donna's mother passed away in her late 70s from breast and pancreatic cancers. Disheartened as she was, Donna wondered if other family members had died of cancer, since her extended family never spoke of such things. She began to ask questions and, startlingly, discovered the answer to her question was, unfortunately, a resounding "yes": five family members had died of cancer, and three of those deaths were from breast cancer.

Realizing she might very well be next, Donna immediately began getting annual mammograms under the care of the same doctor who had taken care of her mother. Sometime in the early 1990s, Donna's doctor discovered two breast calcifications—calcium deposits within the breast tissue, usually benign—and given Donna's family history, her doctor took no chances, performing a biopsy and removing both the calcifications, which were indeed benign. Donna felt truly blessed to escape the trauma of cancer, until her faith was tested...

In 2003, Donna felt God indeed tested her faith—after she almost lost her beloved husband.

Tony Vallone was one of the first 45 victims diagnosed that year in Houston with the West Nile Virus. The time from infection to the appearance of symptoms (the incubation period) is typically between 2 and 15 days. Symptoms may include fever, headaches, fatigue, muscle pain or aches, malaise, nausea, anorexia, vomiting, and rash. Tony's symptoms were severe, with fevers spiking near hyperpyrexia levels, which could have resulted in dire consequences—even death.

Donna was terrified by the sight of Tony's health crumbling drastically before her eyes. She rushed him to the hospital and watched helplessly as the emergency medical staff administered care to his sometimes almost lifeless body. His temperature reached up to 105 degrees.

At the time, Tony received the typical medical treatment for reducing fever, since statistically there was limited data about how to treat severe cases of this disease. Tony's continuous fever never dropped, and the doctors and nurses worked tirelessly at getting the fever down. Surprisingly, nothing was working, and Donna began to pray, saying, "Please God, let Tony's fever break, and put him on the road to recovery. He's just too good a man to die."

Thank goodness for the quick thinking of Nurse Mettie, who quickly changed Tony's fever medication and began utilizing a cooling mechanism to counteract endogenous heat production. This involved placing Tony on an ice bath mattress, with both Donna and Nurse Mettie administering cold packs to his entire body—very possibly saving Tony's life.

Donna felt blessed because she felt God had saved her soulmate's life. This was a significant year in both of their lives, from Tony's near-death experience to his decision to sell five of his restaurants. Then, after three decades, they decided to move Tony's Restaurant to Greenway Plaza. Tony said at the time, "I'm in a place in my life right now where I'm very happy." Later, however, some surprising news would rock his world.

In 2007, Donna's post-mammogram news was not good. A scan had revealed a 0.7-millimeter lump, just broken through a milk duct in Donna's right breast. This time, she received the cruel cancer diagnosis, hearing those awful words, "I am so sorry…"

Donna called Tony in a panic with the horrifying news. Tony was speechless, later saying, "I drove like a maniac to the hospital to be by her side—she needed my reassurance that everything was going to be okay, and I had to comfort her during this scary time." Tony then had the hard job of telling the children their mother's diagnosis. *How can I even put this into words?* he thought. *How can I best protect my family?* "All is going to be fine," he kept reassuring them, but on the inside, he was terrified of the grim possibility that they wouldn't arrest her cancer in time, and fear began to creep into his mindset: *What if…?*

Then came some good news. Donna's cancer was discovered early enough that it was still contained within the breast—in other words, the doctors determined that the cancer was Stage 1, with no metastasis to organs or other parts of the body. Her surgery, still a terrifying process to Donna, with all the what-ifs, entailed only a lumpectomy and allowed her to keep most of her breast. In the hours and days post-surgery, Tony would not leave Donna's side, just in case she needed him. He slept sitting up in a chair holding her hand and made sure Donna could see him if she awoke in the middle of the night. Sounds like the kind of love you'd only read about in Shakespeare.

With the surgery behind her, Donna would spend the next six weeks undergoing radiation therapy and the next five years taking medication. Thank goodness, Donna's quest for answers about her family's medical history gave her—and likely her family and many others—the gift of life for generations to come.

## IMPROVING THE ODDS

*When I am afraid, I put my trust in you. In God, whose word I praise—in God I trust and am not afraid...*
—Psalm 56:3-4 (NIV)

Because Donna's cancer was detected early, she had a full recovery. The longer cancer progresses, however, the more the survival rate drops: for cancer discovered in Stage 4, the five-year survival rate plummets to 22 percent. The five-year observed survival rate refers to the percentage of patients who live at least five years after being diagnosed with cancer, although some patients live beyond those five years.

Early detection continues to be the key to breast cancer survival. For many years, researchers have underscored the importance of early detection (a term now nearly synonymous with optimal survival odds), with journals citing findings epitomized by the following statement: "The risk of metastases and death increases with both breast cancer size at detection and number of axillary lymph nodes involved. Screening aims to improve survival by decreasing the risk of metastases through early detection of breast cancer."

*Cancer never discriminates, the young the old, the hard the soft,*
*You tried to take me, You tried to take my hair, my breast, my life,*
*but I won now cancer-free.*
—Unknown

The radiation treatments were exhausting, and Donna had to endure them for six weeks. To minimize the side effect of fatigue, Donna arranged to receive her treatments in the late afternoon so that she and Tony could go to work every morning and remain for most of the day. "With Tony at my side, I felt like everything was going to be okay,"

Donna says, and by keeping a regular schedule, it took her mind off all the what-ifs.

Donna felt fortunate to attend MD Anderson's radiation treatment facility in Houston for her care. For 2015, it ranked number one for cancer care in the "Best Hospitals" survey published in *U.S. News and World Report* and is widely regarded as among the best cancer hospitals in the United States. After the final radiation treatment, each patient is given the opportunity to ring a bell that signifies completion; this same bell is rung at a later point in time to signify the status of "breast cancer survivor."

Donna recalls how much worse off the other women with stage 2 to 4 cancers seemed; at times, she even felt guilty because she still had her hair. However, "Donna always tried to cheer up the other women with her upbeat persona," says Tony, "and one thing that remained constant was her prayer, every day, for these women to beat cancer just like her." And Donna often sang to relieve her stress, Tony reports, adding, "She has an angelic voice and probably wasn't even aware that her singing helped melt away my stress, too."

## ON MY WAY!

*Ring the bell, three times well, its toll to clearly say, my treatment's done, this course is run, and I am on my way!*
—U.S. Navy Rear Admiral Irve Le Moyne

On August 9, 2007, Donna rang the MD Anderson bell three times for herself and for her family to signify she had beaten breast cancer.

"I'm not sure where I would be without my faith," says Donna. "It's gotten me through some difficult times…and I'm especially grateful to my wonderful husband, Tony, who has loved me through both the tough times and the happy ones." She thanks God for their family unit, which now includes seven grandchildren, ranging in age from late 20s to three years old.

Donna's lesson in her cancer journey was always to remain faithful while traveling on her life's path. She has come to discover that, no matter the journey, faith saw her through—even after losing her beloved grandparents and later her parents, after becoming a widow at age 36, the near death experience of her soulmate, and then after receiving a diagnosis of breast cancer. Donna learned early how fragile life is and she cherishes every moment given on this earth. Moreover, committed to paying it forward, so others may also live. This woman is living proof that miracles and angels do exist—just look closely, and you will see them flying among us every day.

## MAJOR SUCCESS IN...DINING!

The Vallone family is restaurant royalty who practically invented fine dining in Houston. The original Tony's restaurant offered five-star cuisine and joined in Italian food endeavors by the Ciao Bello eatery and Vallone's steakhouse.

The *Houston Business Journal* has referred to Tony Vallone's management of a fine-dining restaurant as analogous to masterpieces performed by major arts organizations: "You have to have consistency. You have to have technique. And then you have to have delivery, where you choreograph the services, the food, and the ambiance," and Tony's "has it all." Tony's celebrated half a century in 2015.

## DONNA'S THOUGHTS ON SUCCESS
- Never be afraid to ask questions, ever!
- Always go with your first instinct.
- Be true to yourself.
- Like yourself—and if you do not, find out why.
- Stay healthy, both spiritually and physically.

- Reach out if you need help.
- Be kind to yourself, especially as you get older.
- Make sure your spouse and family know how important they are to you.
- Enjoy what you are doing, or do something else.
- Don't ever stop communicating.
- Never be afraid to give hugs!

*Age is merely the number of years the world has been enjoying you.*
*—Unknown*

Donna uses her life experiences and influence to shine a light on others who may have been forgotten. With her encouraging words of faith and caring soul, shared with all she meets, Donna exemplifies grace (and, yes, she does like to give *hugs*!).

## Write Your Goals for Success

_____

_____

_____

_____

(Go to www.GodGaveUsWings.com for a free worksheet.)

## PAY IT FORWARD

*Sometimes you are granted more time to shine brighter than you could foresee—and, through your brilliant illumination, you lighten the path so others may see - and you begin to fly higher than you could ever imagine.*
*—Connie Rankin*

Fully aware she has been given the gift of life, Donna Vallone uses this gift to advocate for those without a voice. She uses her life experience as a breast cancer survivor to advocate for early awareness. Donna's warm and soothing personality quickly penetrates others' hearts about the importance of early detection of breast cancer to help save lives. After all, it saved hers.

Donna says she realizes now that she's actually a minority regarding hereditary breast cancer because the majority of women who get breast cancer don't have breast cancer in their families. That's why she is such a staunch supporter for mammograms.

Donna says she has beat breast cancer and feels a cure is imminent. She uses her influence to garner attention as a speaker at numerous fundraising events benefiting early detection programs at the University of Texas, MD Anderson Cancer Center, and the Bobetta Lindig Breast Care Center at Memorial Hermann Memorial City Hospital.

She is a fixture at local fundraising events that advocate for breast cancer awareness, always praying for a cure for future generations. Donna was also a founder, chairperson, and honoree at the Memorial Hermann annual Razzle Dazzle Luncheon. She serves on several boards, including the Memorial Hermann Community Relations Advisory Committee, the Houston West Chamber of Commerce, TEACH, the Advisory Council for the Houston Affiliate of Susan G. Komen for the Cure, the Founding Advisory Committee for the Design Society of Houston Community College, and the Holocaust Museum Houston— the list goes on.

Donna says, "I'm a survivor, but women younger than me have been lost to this disease. That is why I am such an advocate for early detection. If I can save even one life, that's worth it."

This woman is on a mission to help eradicate breast cancer in the next generation. Donna does her part to spread the word that early detection saves lives—hers, theirs, and yours!

## List a Few Ways You Can Help Others

_____

_____

_____

_____

_____

## IMPORTANT INFORMATION ABOUT
## BREAST CANCER RISK FACTORS

If you have any of the risk factors listed below, talk to your doctor about getting these tests more often and adding more tests, including breast MRI (magnetic resonance imaging) and genetic testing. If you are concerned about inherited family syndromes that may cause breast cancer, there is advanced genetic testing to let you know your risk. Anything that increases your chance of getting breast cancer is a risk factor.

These factors include:

- Age: While most cases occur in women 50 or older, breast cancer sometimes develops in women in their 20s. Age is the main risk factor.
- Family history (especially mother, sister, daughter) with ovarian and/or breast cancer.
- Hormones/childbirth: Your risk of breast cancer is higher if you:
  - Had your first period before age 12
  - Began menopause after age 55
  - Never had children
  - Had your first child after age 30
  - Used hormone therapy after menopause
  - Have a history of radiation to the chest area
  - Have previous abnormal breast biopsy results

- ○  Have breast diseases such as atypical hyperplasia or lobular or ductal carcinoma
- ○  Suffered from obesity or weight gain after menopause
- ○  Inherited susceptibility genes BRCA1 and BRCA2, which account for about 5–10 percent of breast cancer cases. Tell your doctor if other women in your family have had breast cancer.

Other breast cancer risk factors include:

- • Oral contraceptive use (birth control pills)
- • Diet high in saturated fats
- • Not getting enough exercise
- • Drinking more than one alcoholic drink a day

Not everyone with risk factors gets breast cancer. However, if you have risk factors, it's a good idea to discuss them with your doctor. Research shows that many cancers can be prevented. Visit http://www.mdanderson.org to learn more.

## BLESSING PRAYER

"My Lord God, I have no idea where I am going. I do not see the road ahead of me. I cannot know for certain where it will end... I will not fear, for You are ever with me, and You will never leave me to face my perils alone." -Thomas Merton.

## NEXT CHAPTER

The next story will take you back to a simpler time when parents allowed their children total freedom to play, entirely unsupervised; the only mandate was to get home in time for dinner. Even a five-year-old played outside then, to roam the neighborhood carefree until the unimaginable happened...

## CHAPTER 10

# Turning *Can't* into *Can*

*Consider it pure joy, my brothers and sisters, whenever you face trials of many kinds, because you know that the testing of your faith produces perseverance*
— James 1:2–3 (NIV)

## LIFE'S TRIALS

Imagine growing up in an era when parents allowed their children the total freedom to play, entirely unsupervised, the only mandate to get home in time for dinner. Even a five-year-old was permitted to play outside then, to roam the neighborhood carefree, fearing only the most minor of consequences—a skinned knee, perhaps, or at most, a bump on the forehead. The late 1950s were a time of what today's society would consider inconceivable childhood freedom.

It was a time when no one had ever heard of video games, or iPads, or even cell phones. Imagine the joy of the weekend—no school! No homework! Children got up, ate their Wheaties, and…played! What sheer fun. Boys raced bikes to see who could conquer that hill first (and likely crash). Girls played with their newly released Barbie dolls and listened to the record player, jamming out to their favorite rock and roll tunes.

One particular Saturday morning, a young, five-year-old girl woke up just like any other day and realized her two irritating sisters were already outside playing. She had the whole house to herself, including both parents' undivided attention. Life was good!

But she soon tired of the semi-solitude. Heading outdoors in search of friends, she instead discovered a lost boy, around two years old, crying for his mother. He was sitting next to a four-foot-high brick wall that separated two subdivisions. Maybe, she thought, he lives on the other side of the wall. She gingerly put the boy on her back and had just begun scaling the wall when—it all happened so fast—she lost her balance and fell down, onto her knees. And at that moment, life changed—drastically.

The girl had landed on a tin can lid partially embedded in the ground. The jagged metal sliced deep into her right knee, shearing through muscle and bone. Only a chunk of flesh held—slightly, at best—the leg in place. From inside the house, her parents heard the blood-curdling scream of a child…was it their child? They rushed outside to find her covered in blood, and her mom hysterically began shouting, "please, someone call an ambulance."

Kneeling beside her daughter, the mother heard only sirens and her child's anguished words, echoing in the still air: "God, I love you, but I love my mother, too!"

God heard her plea. When she arrived at the hospital in her blood-soaked clothes, the emergency room doctor found a miracle: the bleeding had stopped without a tourniquet. The child did not die. Rather, she lived, knowing God performs miracles every day in people's lives if only they believe. That day, her faith saved her life and her limb. (The fact that no tourniquet was applied was a miracle; because back then if a tourniquet was used it usually lead to an amputation.) Her faith gave her a lifelong gift, too: the strength to persevere.

During the first two weeks of her six-week stay in the hospital, the girl noticed that her mother would sometimes leave for an hour at a time. One day, upset, she asked, "But where are you going?" The next thing she knew, she was strapped into a wheelchair and heading to the children's ward. Her mother had been spoon-feeding an eight-year-old girl whose room was in the overcrowded children's ward of the hospital. Sally had suffered burns over 90 percent of her body in a terrible accident from playing with matches. Wrapped like a mummy and in severe pain, the child was also quite alone—her family rarely got to visit because they had to work. Like most children, Sally began missing her parents; she wanted to go home to see them and to play chase with her two brothers. The younger of the two girls suddenly realized just how lucky she was to have her mother by her side. From that time on, she asked everyone who came to visit her to also visit Sally.

Everyone—and there were many—who met Sally wanted her to recover, but that was not to be. Sally's short life would drastically impact this child, who had decided to run on her friend's behalf. In the midst of her deep sorrow, she discovered a new strength—the determination to not only walk, but to run...and to not only run, but to fly, like in her dreams.

During the first four weeks of her hospital stay, the doctors found no sign of nerve attachment in her leg. Each morning when the surgeon dropped by to examine her, he would ask if she could wiggle the big toe peeking out from the end of her full leg cast. The results were always the same—no feeling, no movement. Shortly after losing her friend, things were different. This time, her toe began wriggling back and forth. She watched as her usually solemn doctor, the nurses, staff members, and her family all started jumping up and down with joy.

This early life experience gave her the courage and determination to accomplish things she might have otherwise thought impossible. It took her over a year before she would walk again. She had experienced a trial that would test her faith and produce the endurance she needed to regain this essential life skill. She had learned that when you fall, you have to get back up.

## A RIPPLE EFFECT

Sometimes, we forget that God does not cause bad things to happen to His people. Rather, He carries us through the darkness until we are strong enough to stand once again on our own—and, finally, fly. In her well-known "Footprints" prayer, Margaret Fishback Powers powerfully affirms that God is always with us. In the final lines of the poem, God assures the reader He embraces us most in our times of greatest need: "...when you saw only one set of footprints, it was then that I carried you."

The girl was seven when her father left his family for another woman, an action that hit her 30-year-old mother like a ton of bricks. Her father's leaving shattered her mom's already fragile self-esteem, resurfacing feelings of abandonment by her Dad as a child. This woman's three biggest fears—who would hire someone of her age, with three children and with a minimal education, in an era when women weren't even supposed to work? Those fears were soon realized. With no job or prospect of one, panic began to set in. Perhaps if they moved to another state, things would change. Even better, what if she were to find her long-lost father? Surely, he would help.

Her mother was right. Their lives did change, but for the worse. They plummeted from a middle-class family into poverty, ending up living in a shack—and just as she thought things couldn't get any worse…it did.

This child's mother found her own long-lost father. At the time, he was a violent alcoholic, who loved to fight with both his wife and brother. Her mother, seem pleased with the reunion, introduced him as "This is your real grandfather!" But her daughter rejected the notion. *My real grandfather lives with my grandmother in Georgia*, she kept thinking, *and I want to go home now*. But this would not happen.

Instead, one night as they slept, a distant relative's inappropriate behavior caused the nine-year-old to cry out for help. Thank goodness, her mother rescued the girl before the unthinkable happen.

With nowhere to turn, this child's mother married an illiterate man ten years her junior, one with anger issues. Together, they had a son. But things spiraled downward at a steady pace until her new stepfather beat her mother almost daily in fits of jealousy. Five years into the marriage, in another fit of rage, he pulled out a gun, aimed, and shot, barely missing her mother. Soon afterward, they divorced.

Once again desperate, her mother finally found a job tending bar at a local tavern. Things seemed to go more smoothly for the family until her mother lost her job. Unable to find a steady job, they began moving from place to place, her mother doing whatever she could to feed her children. In the space of one year, the children went to six different schools. Always trying to catch up with their schoolwork, and as they made new friends would move again. The struggle to pay the rent seemed to never end, and there were times they were even homeless.

One night when she was 12, this child cried out to God, "How can you let this happen to my family?" At some point, she would realize that their troubles did not stem from God, but from her parents' poor choices. But for now, she could turn nowhere for comfort but Above.

And yet, no matter how tough the going, God seems to give us earth angels to help us through our times of greatest need. During those agonizing preteen years, there was an oasis, a fourth-grade teacher. Daily, she delivered the same message of inspiration: "Can't never could do anything!" Somehow, she took hope from those words. Using them as her mantra thoughout her life, and sharing them with others.

Later, with a little peer pressure and a whole lot of courage, she quietly and steadily began to teach herself how to ride a bike and swim at the age of 13. Her success in these efforts led to a newfound freedom from fear, fear that had held her back—she had done it! She had succeeded in those quests. On the first day of that realization, she flew like an eagle on her sister's bike.

## TWISTS AND TURNS

*A little belief, A little faith, A little hope is sometimes all we need, to see the light.*
—Charles F. Glassman

Fast-forward and the little girl grew into a woman—an often-scared woman. Her flight rarely followed a straight path; instead, it took many twists and turns, including marriage at age 18 to a person with an addictive personality. One year later, she gave birth to her son and remained in the dysfunctional marriage for over 14 years—until she finally decided enough was enough.

The day her divorce became final was the day her journey of emotional healing began. Now on the road to recovery—and it was not easy, especially since she feared change—it would take many years before she realized such change could be good if she embraced it as a learning experience. Gradually she began transforming into all that God had created her to be.

Finding strength through motivational and self-help books, she listened daily to Zig Ziglar tapes while driving to and from work. One of Ziglar's quotes particularly guided her: "Don't let the mistakes and disappointments of the past control and direct your future." Gradually, she saw how flawed her family's views on life had been...and she realized that she could change her mindset.

## FEAR INTO FAITH

*I can do all this through him who gives me strength.*
—Philippians 4:13 (NIV)

She knew how crippling fear could be; it can prevent you from receiving God's blessings, from sprouting wings and flying to unimaginable heights. As she became more and more confident and less and less afraid, her life took off like a jet plane. Her wings strengthened, her confidence soared, and she began taking greater risks that reaped greater rewards. She is no longer settling for second best; she shot for the stars and got the moon. In her 40s, she met a wonderful man and got married within a year—and, two decades later, he is still my Godsend.

Yes, I am that little girl from so many years ago. As I got stronger, I realized that I had the ability to choose my path, a path that led to one of two doors: (1) let past occurrences label me as a victim, grounding me for life, or (2) turn my life experiences into victories to achieve all things that would allow me to soar.

I chose door number 2 and decided to use all of my life experiences— to repair my broken wings and fly higher than imaginable.

This decision, made years ago, allowed me to step out of fear into a brighter future; instead of a life ruled by fear, I am filled with excitement about the wonder it holds. This decision has also allowed me to fulfill a dream, the dream of owning a company. Moving past my fears has enabled me to achieve significant accomplishments in life, like writing this book.

## BUSINESS

In 2001, I opened my own commercial real estate firm, and by that July, I had become a certified woman-owned company. Soon afterward, I must have gotten some Divine help on my path to success—because I bumped into someone from many years ago. Surprisingly, after sharing my good news, this mere acquaintance suggested I represent him in his office expansion. Little did I know that his company had grown from 6,000 square feet of office space to more than 36,000 sq ft!

What a great first client: my fees earned enough for me to establish a nice office and, ultimately, to hire a secretary and two leasing agents.

## AWARDS AND RECOGNITIONS

Since starting my company, I've been blessed with numerous awards for both my business success and my volunteerism. They are all very special to me, but three stand out the most. In 2006, my company was recognized as a Top Business Star by the Women's Business Enterprise National Council for our excellent customer service and community involvement. This award gave me the opportunity to be a guest at the White House. Then, in 2013, my firm was recognized as the Top Fastest Growing Women-Owned Businesses, by the Houston Business Journal; this was the same year I was named as a Woman of Influence by the Real Estate Forum for my dedication to helping other women succeed in commercial real estate.

Here's one of my greatest rewards: I get to control my destiny and, through my success, I get to pay it forward in a bigger way. John F. Kennedy paraphrasing from the Bible in Luke 12:48 once said: "For of those to whom much is given, much is required." This book allows me the opportunity to share my life experiences, along with those of other women—to show you there are no obstacles you can't fly over if you believe.

> *The woman was given the two wings of a great eagle, so that she might fly to the place prepared for her…*
> —Revelation 12:14 (NIV)

## CONNIE'S THOUGHTS ON SUCCESS

- Don't be afraid to take chances.
- My greatest successes came from my greatest risks.
- When you fall down, you must get up.
- Value yourself, or others won't.
- Sometimes, your darkest hours will result in your brightest light.
- Don't ever give up on your dreams…that big opportunity could be just around the corner.
- Don't take "no" for an answer. It may be "no" today, but it could be "yes" tomorrow.
- One key to success is gentle persistence without being a pest.
- Seek mentors to guide you along your path, and mentor others.
- Never stop learning—because knowledge is power.
- Toot your own horn, or you won't get tooted.

### *Write Your Goals for Success*

_____

_____

_____

_____

_____

(Go to www.GodGaveUsWings.com for a free worksheet.)

## PAY IT FORWARD

*In the midst of a very severe trial, their overflowing joy and their extreme poverty welled up in rich generosity. For I testify that they gave as much as they were able, and even beyond their ability. Entirely on their own, they urgently pleaded with us for the privilege of sharing in this service to the Lord's people. And they exceeded our expectations: They gave themselves first of all to the Lord, and then by the will of God also to us.*
                    —2 Corinthians 8:2–5 (NIV)

My life's motto is to strive to be bigger than myself. It's important for me to find ways to make things better for others. For this reason, I founded CRES over a decade and a half ago, to act as an advocate for companies needing office space. This allows me to control my destiny while contributing to the success of others. I am pleased to say my company's mission is bigger than our bottom line, so I have incorporated a giving-back program as part of my company's business model. At the year's end, a donation is made to several nonprofit organizations that help educate and empower others to increase their chances of achieving success.

There have, of course, been those times where I especially felt the need to turn to God for comfort and strength. One such day, under pressure and troubled, I asked God, "What has happened to my joy?" Almost immediately, the inner voice reminded me that joy is action without expectation of reward. The answer was clear: to be bigger than myself. Because of this, I am passionate about helping other women achieve their dreams, including owning a business.

Therefore, I have become the driving force in creating the Giving Tree, a scholarship program united with the Women's Business Enterprise Alliance, a nonprofit organization dedicated to promoting women in business. This program provides needed scholarships and mentorship for new startup businesses that may otherwise fail without the Giving Tree's support.

In 2016, I founded Bridge Literacy Now (www.BridgeLiteracyNow. org), a nonprofit dedicated to improving the lives of women and children to eliminate the "poor child, poor reader" effect. The organization donates books and provides educational programs for women who are enrolled in a GED program, to become self-sufficient. I believe that if you educate moms, they are better equipped to ensure their children become better readers—decreasing the social disparity caused by lack of education.

### List a Few Ways You Can Help Others

_____

_____

_____

_____

_____

## BLESSING PRAYER

My prayer is that God, in His genius, will inspire those who read these stories to go on to write their own stories—stories about how they, too, have overcome obstacles in their lives, grown strong wings, and learned to soar. Amen.

Take action today…it's never too late to fly!

# Conclusion

Attitudes about God have slightly changed over the past six decades. The 8 percent of people surveyed in a Gallup poll who report they are undecided or do not believe in God are largely young liberal Americans and those living in the east. Trends in recent decades indicate that only 1 in 10 Americans say they don't have a formal religious identity. However, 92 percent of the respondents stated that they do believe in God, and this is a clear indication that God's not dead! Willie Robertson says it best: "Rumors of God's death have been greatly exaggerated."

The 10 women who have graciously shared their stories in this book come from diverse ethnic and socioeconomic groups and, in some cases, have little in common, except their belief in God.

Do you want to know how to live in faith? Lose the fear by believing all things are possible with I AM.

My prayer is that after reading *God Gave Us Wings* your wings have grown stronger, allowing you to rise higher than you ever imagined. I would love to hear how these stories have affected your life at www. GodGaveUsWings.com.

# Frequently Asked Questions

*The writing of this book was done in a storytelling manner involving some historical research.*

*Q. Why did you write this book?*
After almost losing my commercial real estate firm as a result of the recession, I became consumed with making money. I lost all emotions—no tears, no laughter, and especially no joy…just emptiness. Then one day, in desperation, I cried out for God to give me back my joy. His answer was unexpected—the message became crystal clear for me to step out in faith and use my life experiences to show others how to do the same.

*Q. How did you identify the women to include in the book?*
During the entire two-year process of writing this book, I prayed every day before writing. This included asking God for divine guidance in identifying the types of stories that required the greatest faith.

Oprah Winfrey was the first person whose name immediately came to mind during prayer, and she was by far the one that took the most faith. Shortly afterward, I learned that Oprah was scheduled to come to my hometown for the Life You Want Weekend. This was my big chance for us to meet. But how? The VIP tickets were sold out. Who could help? There were only five days left before the event, and it would take a miracle. Just a few days remained when a message popped up saying, "you've got mail from *OWN Magazine*." They were having a drawing for tickets to the show—and guess what? I won! Not only did I win the tickets, but someone else also got me a meeting with Oprah! Here's the exciting news: She gave me her blessing to include her powerful story in the book. However, Oprah's blessing did not include a personal interview; instead, I had to perform extensive research to gather information about her life to write her story.

So, one story down, and nine to go—who would be the second chapter? It was the Fourth of July, and we decided to go to Oklahoma to visit family. During this impromptu outing, I heard about a beautiful immigrant named Keo from Laos, whose family found God during their escape to America. Keo, a realtor, agreed to meet with me the next day during an open house. It turned out that no one showed up but us— and I jumped at the opportunity to interview her on the spot. Since then, we have stayed in contact with each other.

The third chapter is about a woman named Sue, whom I've admired for years. She's been my business coach and loyal friend. This lady travels all over the world providing coaching, speaking, and organizational training for major corporations. I got lucky when Sue agreed to share her story for the book. The interview took over four hours and discussed how she overcame verbal abuse and feelings of childhood abandonment. She didn't realize how many old feelings that she had buried for years would erupt during the interview. It was essentially the first time she got to bare all, and she said it felt good.

The fourth chapter was my toughest to write, because it was a young lady who has worked for me for years and about whom I care deeply. She had never fully revealed the depth of her childhood pain over all those years. Lilly's interview was different because she wrote her story for me to read. She was surprised by how healing it felt to write everything down on paper. I am in complete admiration of this young woman's journey to move out of fear into faith.

It was then time to write the next chapter, about a female veteran. A Google search popped up Kendra's name on the Helping a Hero website. It would take four months for me to finally make contact with her through a Facebook message. She agreed to share her story, and so I was off to Savannah, Georgia, for an interview. This turned out to be a life-changing event for us both. This young lady suffered from PTSD and now was going to relive her battle story. It took two days to complete her sometimes-emotional interview. The second day went much better, and she felt good about sharing her story to help others. Indeed, right after finishing Kendra's interview, I learned that my mother had passed away in her sleep, and Kendra consoled me during my grief.

Halfway through writing the book, it was time for me to interview my mentor and friend Donna Cole. She is a very successful business owner who travels all over the world but always finds time to help others. She agreed to be in the book because she wanted to show how you can rise up no matter the circumstances. She is a Japanese-American who lived through World War II and often experienced harsh treatment for being different. Her philanthropic nature has helped thousands reach success.

For Chapter Seven, I took off again to meet a young female veteran hurt during boot camp, who subsequently discovered that her life mission was to help prevent teen pregnancies. She initially was set to be the veteran in the book until I heard her heartfelt story about overcoming the effects of teen pregnancy. She later founded a nonprofit called Lilies and Reeds to present an alternative lifestyle for teens.

The book was 75 percent completed, in Chapter Eight, when I approached a local celebrity, Deborah Duncan, the host of *Good Morning Houston*, to be in the book. Interestingly, all of the interviews up to that point had been completely different, and hers was no exception. The interview took place at the TV station, in her office, and it took about two hours to complete. On a few occasions, she broke out into a song and laughed because wasn't sure how I would put that into writing. Deborah has a huge personality and was a delight to interview. She would introduce me to the next person in the book.

I was now entering the home stretch with writing the ninth chapter, and I knew it was to be a cancer survivor. Deborah Duncan knew just the woman and introduced me to Donna Vallone, who is considered restaurant royalty, as the owner's wife of Tony's which offers five-star cuisine in Houston, Texas. Donna's interview was conducted at Tony's in the wine room, at a large table. Halfway through the interview, we had to move to a smaller room to accommodate customers and moved to a smaller room. Donna is a very humble woman and loves talking about everyone else but herself—so much so that I had to interview her husband, Tony, to find out more about Donna. I loved their energy and how much they love each other after being married for many years.

Next, I had to write the toughest story: about my life. It wasn't easy sharing my personal life with the world, especially how we went from middle-class America to plummeting into poverty. Like Lilly, I wrote a draft copy first and rewrote it several times before arriving at a final draft. *Wow*, what a healing process: the exercise of writing helped heal old wounds from my childhood and filled my heart with love and forgiveness. These women trusted me with their life stories to share with the world, all because we want to show others through example that all things are possible if you trust in I AM.

*Q. How has your life changed since writing God Gave Us Wings?*

A few years ago, my life was all about making money and growing my commercial real estate business. It wasn't about living a fulfilling life with my church, family, and friends. Today, my company is still important—I am traveling more for both business and the book—but I also have a rewarding life outside of work as well. I take time for church, volunteerism, family, and friends, and most of all, to laugh. This book has made me a better person, and I pray it will give you hope for the future to fly, too.

# Afterword

Have you ever felt lost, empty, and joyless? I did a few years ago after almost losing my company during the recession. I became consumed with making money, and to be frank, the only joy I experienced was in closing sales. Sadly, it wasn't spent living in fulfilling relationships with my family, friends, and community.

How had I reached this point in my life? To the outside world, I looked like I had it all figured out, but inside, I was completely emotionless, feeling more like a walking zombie than a living human being.

One day in sheer desperation, I cried out for God to give me back my joy. His answer wasn't what I expected. It became crystal clear that I was to write a book called God Gave Us Wings to empower others to move past their fear into faith. I said, God, I'm not the one and began negotiating with God. That was my first mistake: you never, ever try to negotiate with God! The next thing I heard was that Oprah's story was to be included in the book. Now, I thought, Really, is this a Divine mission or the devil playing a joke? I totally dismissed the whole idea and starting laughing, believing the whole thing was just a figment of my imagination. That was the second mistake: you never, ever laugh at God.

I went on with my daily rituals, which included taking a shower, and I starting laughing again, thinking about how on earth I would ever get to meet Oprah. I would have a better chance of meeting the president. That was the third mistake: never, ever question God. The next thing I heard from my inner voice was, I AM!

As you can imagine, I fell to my knees, crying hysterically, yelling out loud: "Yes…yes…You are!" Thank goodness, I wasn't in the bathtub, or I might have drowned.

Fast-forward: I've met Oprah, and she gave me her blessing for her story to be in the book. If I had not listened to my inner voice, I would not be writing this book on how you can move past your fear into faith to accomplish great things in your life, too.

God shows up and shows up big!

# Acknowledgments

The truth is that by the grace of God and the people in my life made this book become a reality. So many individuals helped me and to whom I owe my sincere appreciation and gratitude.

First, I want to thank all the incredible women for sharing their journey to success, and for Oprah Winfrey for giving me her blessing to include her amazing story, as well. David L.Hancock, Megan Malone, Terry Whalin and everyone at Morgan James Publishing for believing in me and in the mission of empowering others through God's message of hope, love, and faith. I want to also thank my editor Debora Holmes with Inspiration for Writers for her creativity and Lori Paximadis for getting the content to where it is today. Thanks to Dawn Magnan with n8 Solution for her marketing guidance every step of the way, along with Donna Rosenstein for the many brainstorming sessions. Thanks to Chris Bridge, author and ordained minister, for helping write the blessing prayers. I am especially thankful for Ileana Leija, who works with me at CRES and Associates, for the tireless hours she committed to this project, and for sharing her incredible story. Steve Harrison and his excellent team at Bradley Communication for their guidance in showing me how to make this book a best seller, and a special shout out for Rose George for her special friendship. A big bear hug goes to my husband, Don, for his unwavering support, especially in picking up the slack while I was writing almost nonstop for this book. Thanks also, to my beloved son Shane, and my second set of wonderful children, all my grandchildren, and friends for their encouragement and support in completing this project of love.

This is where I wish there were room to add the thousands of other people I can think of who have helped make this book a reality. I simply ask you to forgive the broad strokes. I want to thank the Women's Business Enterprise Alliance and the Women's Business Enterprise National Council for supporting women-owned businesses like mine. And to the all of the great people who have been spreading the word about me who may or may not even know me personally, you all are amazing, and I thank you from the bottom of my heart!

# References

**CHAPTER 1**

"African American History." Black History in America. Accessed November 14, 2014. http://www.myblackhistory.net/history.htm.

"African American Roots." Black History in America. Accessed November 14, 2014. http://www.myblackhistory.net/Roots.htm.

"African Americans." Wikipedia. Last modified May 16, 2016 (3:38 pm). Accessed November 14, 2014. https://en.wikipedia.org/wiki/African_Americans.

Anderson, Erica Lee. "Mississippi Freedom Democratic Party." BlackPast.org. Accessed November 14, 2014. http://www.blackpast.org/aah/mississippi-freedom-democratic-party.

Andre, Claire, Manuel Velasquez, and Tim Mazur. "Affirmative Action: Twenty five Years of Controversy." Santa Clara University. Accessed November 14, 2014. https://legacy.scu.edu/ethics/publications/iie/v5n2/affirmative.html.

andrewkim96. "The Hardships of Oprah Winfrey." People (blog). July 20, 2011. Accessed November 14, 2014. http://www.godsfighter3. blogspot.com/2011/07/hardships-of-oprah-winfrey.html.

"Biography." Oprah Winfrey: Role Model (blog). Accessed November 14, 2014. http://oprahwinfreygamechanger.weebly.com/biography. html.

Carr, Everette. "Leon Turner Trial." Attala County, Mississippi. Accessed November 14, 2014. http://attala-county-history-genealogy.org/court2.html.

Carrillo, Carmel. "'Oprah's Roots' is part biography, part genealogy." Chicago Tribune. January 24, 2007. Accessed November 8, 2014. http://articles.chicagotribune.com/2007-01-24/ features/0701230288_1_girls-in-south-africa-african-american-lives-oprah-winfrey.

"Civil Rights Movement." United States History. Accessed September 27, 2014. http://www.u-s-history.com/pages/h2876.html.

Deutsch, Stephanie. "Oprah's and My Roots." You Need A Schoolhouse (blog). Accessed November 8, 2014. http://www. youneedaschoolhouse.com/stephanies-blog/oprahs-and-my-roots/.

"Early Childhood Development." UNICEF. Accessed November 14, 2014. http://www.unicef.org/earlychildhood/.

EUR "Oprah, Bishop Jakes, Chris Tucker Trace Roots on PBS." Dallas Black. January 31, 2006. Accessed December 2014. http://www. dallasblack.com/entertainment/newversionrootspbs/forum.

Frazier, Karen. "Charities of Oprah Winfrey." Love to Know. Accessed June 25, 2014. http://charity.lovetoknow.com/Charities_of_ Oprah_Winfrey.

Fry, Elizabeth. "A Childhood Biography of Oprah Winfrey." About Entertainment. Last modified December 10, 2014. http://oprah. about.com/od/oprahbiography/p/oprahchildhood.htm.

"The History of the Oprah Winfrey Leadership Academy for Girls—South Africa." About Entertainment. Accessed June 25, 2014. http://oprah.about.com/od/philanthropy/p/leadershipacad.htm.

"A Look into the Personal Life of Oprah Winfrey." About Entertainment. Last modified November 25, 2014. http://oprah.about.com/od/oprahbiography/p/personallife.htm.

"An Overview and History of Oprah's O Ambassadors." About Entertainment. Accessed June 25, 2014. http://oprah.about.com/od/philanthropy/p/oambassadors.htm.

Gale, Thomson. "Oprah Winfrey." Encyclopedia.com. 2007. http://www.encyclopedia.com/topic/Oprah_Winfrey.aspx.

Gates, H. L., Jr. *Finding Oprah's Roots*. New York: Crown Publishers, 2007.

Gurian, A. "How Important Are the First Three Years of Baby's Life?" Child Study Center. Accessed September 27, 2014. http://www.aboutourkids.org/articles/how_important_are_first_three_years_baby039s_life.

"Language and Communication: The First Five Years." Accessed September 27, 2014. http://www.aboutourkids.org/articles/lanuage_communication_five_years.

"Hattie Mae Presley 1899–1963." Ancestry Accessed November 25, 2014. http://www.ancestry.com/genealogy/records/hattie-mae-presley_63929859

Imbornoni, Ann-Marie. "Women's Right's Movement in the U.S." Accessed November 14, 2014. http://infoplease.com/spot/womenstimeline1.html.

"Is Oprah Winfrey's Grandmother Still Alive?" Yahoo! Answers. Accessed November 25, 2014. https://answers.yahoo.com/question/index?qid=20080519154943AACbKtl.

Johnson, Gwendolyn. "Oprah Winfrey." Mississippi Writers and Musicians. Accessed November 14, 2014. http://www. mswritersandmusicians.com/mississippi-writers/oprah-winfrey.

"July 11, 1954." The University of Southern Mississippi. Accessed November 14, 2014. http://usm.edu/crdp/html/cd/citizens.htm.

Kindig, Jessie. "Freedom Summer (June–August 1964)." BlackPast. org. Accessed November 14, 2014. http://www.blackpast.org/aah/freedom-summer-june-august-1964.

"Kosciusko, Mississippi." City-Data.com. Accessed November 14, 2014. http://www.city-data.com/city/Kosciusko-Mississippi. html#b.

"Kosciusko, Mississippi." Wikipedia. Last modified May 12, 2016 (11:37 pm). https://en.wikipedia.org/wiki/Kosciusko,_Mississippi.

"Mississippi History Timeline, 1954." Mississippi History Timeline. Accessed November 14, 2014. http://mdah.state.ms.us/timeline/zone/1954/.

"Oprah Winfrey." Netglimse. 2013. Accessed September 2014. http://www.netglimse.com/celebs/pages/oprah_winfrey/index.shtml.

"Oprah Winfrey." Wikipedia. Last modified May 17, 2016 (1:25 pm). Accessed June 25, 2014. https://en.wikipedia.org/wiki/African_Americans.

"Oprah Winfrey: Biography." Urban Hustler (blog). Accessed September 2014. http://oprah.urbanhustler.com/biography/.

"Oprah Winfrey Biography." Academy of Achievement. Last modified August 31, 2015. http://www.achievement.org/autodoc/page/win0bio-1.

"Oprah Winfrey Biography." Biography Channel UK. Accessed June 25, 2014. http://thebiographychannel.co.uk/biographies/oprah-winfrey.html.

"Oprah Winfrey Biography." Biography.com. Accessed June 25, 2014. http://www.biography.com/people/oprah-winfrey-9534419.

"Oprah Winfrey Biography." Encyclopedia of World Biography. Accessed September 2014. http://www.notablebiographies.com/We-Z/Winfrey-Oprah.html.

"Oprah Winfrey Biography." People.com. Accessed June 25, 2014. http://www.people.com/people/oprah_winfrey/biography.

"Oprah Winfrey Biography." TVDuck.com. Accessed September 26, 2014. http://tvduck.com/oprah-winfrey-celebrity-photos.html.

"Oprah Winfrey Finds Her Roots Thanks to DNA Test." International Biosciences. Accessed November 08, 2014. https://www.ibdna.com/black-americans/.

"Oprah Winfrey Interview—Academy of Achievement." Academy of Achievement. Last modified December 05, 2016. http://www.achievement.org/achiever/oprah-winfrey/.

"Oprah Winfrey Interview—Academy of Achievement." Academy of Achievement—Print Review. Last modified July 13, 2012 (7:32 pm). http://www.achievement.org/autodoc/printmember/win0int-1.

"Oprah Winfrey's Notable Quotations." About Entertainment. http://oprah.about.com/od/oprahquotes/.

"Oprah Winfrey's Surprising DNA Test." Ancestry. Accessed May 14, 2014. http://blogs.ancestry.com/cm/2014/05/27/the-surprising-facts-oprah-winfrey-learned-about-her-dna/.

Powell, Kimberly. "Ancestry of Oprah Winfrey—Fourth Generation." About Parenting. http://genealogy.about.com/od/aframertrees/p/oprah_two.htm.

"Ancestry of Oprah Winfrey." About Parenting. http://genealogy.about.com/od/aframertrees/p/oprah_winfrey.htm.

Presco, Jon. "Oprah Winfrey and the Rosamond Family Roots in Kosciusko." Templar history (blog). March 13, 2008 (6:31 pm). http://permalink.gmane.org/gmane.culture.templar.rosemont/2206.

Sean, Peter. "Oprah Winfrey—Biography." IMDb. Accessed June 25, 2014. http://www.imdb.com/name/nm0001856/bio.

Smith, Stacy Jenel. "Oprah and Recently Found Sister—Where Are They Now?" AARP (blog). July 28, 2013. http://blog.aarp.org/2013/07/28/oprah-recently-found-sister-where-are-they-now/.

Stasi, Linda. "Oprah's 'Roots' Showing." New York Post (blog). January 24, 2007 (10:00 am). http://nypost.com/2007/01/24/oprahs-roots-showing/.

U.S. Census Bureau. "Kosciusko City, Mississippi—Community Facts." United States Census Bureau. Accessed November 14, 2014. http://factfinder.census.gov/faces/nav/jsf/pages/community_facts.xhtml.

"Kosciusko City, Mississippi—QuickFacts." United States Census Bureau. Accessed November 14, 2014. http://www.census.gov/quickfacts/table/PST045215/2838320,00.

"Winfrey, Oprah (1954–)." Encyclopedia.com. 2002. Accessed September 26, 2014. http://www.encyclopedia.com/article-1G2-2591309941/winfrey-oprah-1954.html.

Winfrey, Oprah. "What I Know for Sure." O Magazine. July 19, 2008. Accessed April 2014. http://www.oprah.com/omagazine/What-I-Know-for-Sure-Oprah-Winfrey.

"Women's History in America." Women's International Center. 1995. http://www.wic.org/misc/history.htm.

xpsantos. "Early Life." Oprah Winfrey Biography (blog). July 21, 2007 (7:55 pm). http://oprahbiography.blogspot.com/2007/07/early-life.html.

## CHAPTER 2

"Fifty Years on, Impact of America's 'Secret War' Lingers." World Bulletin. May 19, 2014 (10:48 am). http://www.worldbulletin.net/haber/136676/50-years-on-impact-of-americas-secret-war-lingers.

Bonner, Mitchell. "A Visit to the Laotian Refugee Camp at Nong Khai Thailand." Online Archive of California. http://www.oac.cdlib.org/view?docId=hb900008z5&brand=oac4&doc.view=entire_text.

"Can You Explain the Effect of the Vietnam War on Laos and Cambodia?" answerparty.com. Retrieved August 3, 2014. http://answerparty.com/questions/answer/can-you-explain-the-effect-on-the-vietnam-war-on-laos-and-combodia.

Crossette, Barbara. "Laotian Refugees Crowd Thai Camp." *New York Times*. June 23, 1985. http://www.nytimes.com/1985/06/23/world/laotian-refugees-crowd-thai-camp.html.

"Hmong Resistance in Laos 1975–1992." Onwar https://www.onwar.com/aced/chrono/c1900s/yr70/flaos1977.htm.

"Laos: History." Infoplease. http://infoplease.com/encyclopedia/world/laos-history.html.

"Laos and Vietnam War." Olive-Drab. Last modified October 12, 2011. http://olive-drab.com/od_history_vietnam_laos.php.

Mattson, A. "Hmong Fighters Still Hiding in the Jungles of Laos." Vietnam and After (blog). December 18, 2007 (7:37 pm). http://wcownews.typepad.com/Vietnam/2007/12/hmong-fighters.html.

Owen, Lewis. "Mekong River." Encyclopedia Brittantica. Last modified January 29, 2016. Accessed August 5, 2014. http://www.britannica.com/place/Mekong-River.

"Remembering the Vietnamese Exodus." Refugee Camps (blog). Last modified July 2014. http://refugeecamps.net.

Savada, Andrea Matles, and Donald P. Whitaker. *Laos: A Country Study*. Washington, DC: Federal Research Division, Library of Congress, 1995. http://countrystudies.us/laos/93.htm, http://countrystudies.us/laos/50.htm.

Somnuk Phongsouvanh. "An open letter to the World Community." Liberal Democratic Newsletter (blog). March 27, 2006. http://www.laofreedom.com/2006/03/.

Staines, T. "Journey to Freedom." *Mosaic Mission* (May 2011): 16–18.

"Thailand—The Indochinese Refugee Question." Country Data. http://www.country-data.com/cgi-bin/query/r-13736.html.

## CHAPTER 3

Domel, Julie. "Kids Offer to Help Milk and Ice Fund." My San Antonio (blog). May 3, 2012 (11:15 am). Accessed October 13, 2014. http://www.blog.mysanantonio.com/vault/2012/05/kids-offer-help-to-milk-and-ice-fund/.

"Lipedema." Wikipedia. Accessed September 16, 2014. https://en.wikipedia.org/wiki/Lipedema.

"Women's Body Image and BMI." Mirror-mirror.org. 2016. http://www.mirror-mirror.org.

## CHAPTER 4

Butler, Alia. "Side Effects of Abuse." Livestrong.com. August 2013. Accessed October 11, 2014. http://www.livestrong.com/article/195719-side-effects-of-abuse/.

Carnes, David. "The Mental and Emotional Abuse of Children." Livestrong.com. August 2013. Accessed October 11, 2014. http://www.livestrong.com/article/243081-the-mental-emotional-abuse-of-children/.

Castro, Roberto, Corinne Peek-Asa, and Augustin Ruiz. "Violence Against Women in Mexico: A Study of Abuse Before and During Pregnancy." *American Journal of Public Health* 93, no. 7 (July 2003): 1110–1116. http://www.ncbi.nlm.nih.gov/pmc/articles/PMC1447918/.

Child Welfare Information Gateway. "Long-Term Consequences of Child Abuse and Neglect." Children's Bureau. 2013. https://www.childwelfare.gov/pubs/factsheets/long-term-consequences/.

Gluck, Samantha. "Effects of Domestic Violence, Domestic Abuse (On Women and Children)." Healthy Place. July 27, 2012. Accessed October 11, 2014. http://www.healthyplace.com/abuse/domestic-violence/effects-of-domestic-violence-domestic-abuse-on-women-and-children/.

Holly, Kellie. "Effects of Verbal Abuse on Children, Women and Men." Healthy Place. July 30, 2012. Accessed June 28, 2013. http://www.healthyplace.com/abuse/verbal-abuse/effects-of-verbal-abuse-on-children-women-and-men/.

"Long-Term Effects of Domestic Violence." The Clark County Prosecuting Attorney. Accessed October 11, 2014. http://www.clarkprosecutor.org/html/domviol/effects.htm.

Tracy, Natasha. "What Is Battered Woman, Battered Wife, Syndrome?" Healthy Place. July 27, 2012. Accessed June 28, 2013. http://www.healthyplace.com/abuse/domestic-violence/what-is-battered-woman-battered-wife-syndrome/.

## CHAPTER 5

Barajas, Eric. "War Veteran Honored with Gift of Home." ABC. February 27, 2012 (4:12 pm). http://abc13.com/archive/8560472/.

"HelpingaHero.org." Black Tie Magazine. Accessed November 9, 2014. http://www.blacktiemagazine.com/US_Society/HelpingAHero.htm.

Huddleston, Scott. "Seg4Vets program brings mobility, healing." My San Antonio (blog). May 19, 2011 (12:44 am). http://www.mysanantonio.com/news/local/military/article/Segs4Vets-program-brings-mobility-healing-1385828.php.

"M23." Hero Flight—Five One Zero. April 29, 2012. http://www.ves4vets.com/?page_id=455.

Meireles, Tania. "The Story behind the Photo, CPL Kendra Coleman." AW2 Blog. April 29, 2011 (12:12 pm). http://aw2.armylive. dodlive.mil/2011/04/the-story-behind-the-photo-cpl-kendra-coleman/.

"SGT (Ret.) Kendra Coleman." Helping a Hero. http://helpingahero. org/our-heroes/sgt-ret-kendra-coleman.

Sudhalter, Michael. "Freedom's Price: Wounded Veteran Says She'd 'Do It Again' to Defend America." Sugar Land Sun. July 17, 2012 (5:37 pm). http://www.yourhoustonnews.com/sugar_land/ living/freedom-s-price-wounded-veteran-says-she-d-do-it/article_ b62eca2a-d068-11e1-9c81-0019bb2963f4.html.

## CHAPTER 6

Cole, Donna Fujimoto. Interview by Maddy Bullard and Saima Toppa. June 1, 2012. Rice University. https://scholarship.rice.edu/ handle/1911/64848.

Davis, B. "Donna Fujimoto Cole—Cole Chemical and Distributing." *Small Business Today Magazine* (October 2013): 6–7.

"Japanese-American Internment." U.S. History. Accessed July 1, 2014. http://www.ushistory.org/us/51e.asp.

Rojas, Paulina. "Honoring Vets, Mentoring Women." *Houston Chronicle*. March 21, 2014. Accessed July 6, 2014. http://www. houstonchronicle.com/about/houston-gives/article/Honoring-vets-mentoring-women-5338792.php.

## CHAPTER 7

Cummins, Jackie. "Causes of Teenage Pregnancy." What to Expect (blog). http://whattoexpect.com/wom/pregnancy/causes-of-teenage-pregnancy-and-ways-to-prevent-it.aspx.

"Graduation, Reality, and Dual-Role Skills." State of Washington Office of Superintendent of Public Instruction. Accessed January

12, 2015. http://www.k12.wa.us/CareerTechEd/GRADSProgram. aspx.

"Oklahoma Adolescent Reproductive Health Facts." U.S. Department of Health and Human Services. Accessed January 11, 2015. http:// www.hhs.gov/ash/oah/adolescent-health-topics/reproductive-health/fact-sheets/state.html?s=oklahoma.

"Teen Pregnancy Prevention." National Conference of State Legislatures. Last modified April 29, 2016. http://www.ncsl.org/ research/health/teen-pregnancy-prevention.aspx.

"Teens." Lilies and Reeds Society. Accessed January 11, 2015. http:// liliesandreedssociety.org/teens.

"What Are the Causes of Teenage Pregnancy?" Healthcare Veda Ezine. March 4, 2009. http://www.healthcareveda.com/post/Causes-of-Teenage-Pregnancy.aspx.

"What Are the Causes of Teenage Pregnancy?" SpeedyRemedies.com. September 1, 2010. http://www.speedyremedies.com/what-are-the-causes-of-teenage-pregnancy.html.

"Who We Are." Lilies and Reeds Society. Accessed January 15, 2015. http://liliesandreedssociety.org/who-we-are.

## CHAPTER 8

Anzaldua, Linda Miller. "Debra Duncan's Wedding." *H-Texas Magazine.* January 1, 2002 (12:01 am). http://htexas.com/ demo/2002/01/debra-duncans-wedding/.

"Exclusive Interview with TV's Deborah Duncan." Health Fitness Revolution. May 8, 2013. Accessed August 12, 2014. http://www. healthfitnessrevolution.com/exclusive-interview-with-tvs-deborah-duncan/.

Grossman, Wendy. "Heir Time." *Houston Press.* February 15, 2001 (4:00 am). http://www.houstonpress.com/news/heir-time-6567287.

KHOU Staff. "Eleven Questions with *Great Day* Host Deborah Duncan." KHOU. 2010. Accessed http://www.khou.com/story/news/2014/07/12/11398446/.

"Living in Taiwan." ESLDewey. http://www.esldewey.com.tw/living.php.

Saxton, Melanie. "A Chat with TV Host Deborah Duncan." May 1, 2013. Houston Lifestyles and Homes. http://houstonlifestyles.com/deborah-duncan/.

## CHAPTER 9

"American Cancer Society Recommendation for Early Breast Cancer Detection in Women without Breast Symptoms." American Cancer Society. Last modified October 20, 2015. http://www.cancer.org/cancer/breastcancer/moreinformation/breastcancerearlydetection/breast-cancer-early-detection-acs-recs.

Balke, Jeff, and Nathan Lindstrom. "You Want It, You Got It." Houstonia. November 3, 2015 (12:00 am). http://www.houstoniamag.com/articles/2015/11/3/interview-tony-vallone-restaurant-business-november-2015.

"Breast Cancer Facts." University of Texas MD Anderson Cancer Center. Accessed September 11, 2015. https://www.mdanderson.org/cancer-types/breast-cancer/breast-cancer-facts.html.

"Breast Cancer Survival Rates, by Stage." American Cancer Society. Accessed September 11, 2015. http://www.cancer.org/cancer/breastcancer/detailedguide/breast-cancer-survival-by-stage.

"Breast—MD Anderson Moon Shots." University of Texas MD Anderson Cancer Center. Accessed September 11, 2015. http://www.cancermoonshots.org/cancer-types/breast/.

"Life Saver: Donna Vallone Advocates for Women's Health." *Absolutely Memorial*. October 2015. https://issuu.com/absolutelymemorial/docs/memorial-october-2015/2.

Mapes, Diane. "Say What? Eight Things You Shouldn't—and Should— Say to a Cancer Patient." Hutch News. October 30, 2013. https://www.fredhutch.org/en/news/center-news/2013/10/what-not-to-say-to-a-cancer-patient.html.

Saadatmand, Sepideh, et al. "Influence of Tumor Stage at Breast Cancer Detection on Survival in Modern Times." *British Medical Journal* 2105;351(h4901).

"The University of Texas MD Anderson Cancer Center." National Cancer Institute. Accessed September 11, 2015. http://www.cancer.gov/research/nci-role/cancer-centers/find/mdanderson.

"University of Texas MD Anderson Cancer Center." Wikipedia. Accessed September 11, 2015. https://en.wikipedia.org/wiki/University_of_Texas_MD_Anderson_Cancer_Center.

Note: Throughout this book, there are several Bible verses used from different versions and duty free quotes from www.oldquotes.com or from other open records.

# About the Author

Connie Rankin has 35 years of executive, professional experience working with Fortune 500 companies, small businesses, educational institutions, and non-profits. She is the president of an award-winning commercial real estate firm and a former Vice President and board chair of the Women's Business Enterprise Alliance and Texas Executive Women. Connie was honored as a Woman of Influence by the National Real Estate Forum and as one of Houston's 50 Most Influential Women of 2016. Her broad life experiences uniquely qualify her as an expert on various women's issues and the challenges facing women in the workplace and beyond. She wrote God Gave us Wings to motivate readers to move out of fear and into faith.

Connie's passion is mentoring women, entrepreneurs, leaders and people from all walks of life on how to achieve success. A sought-after conference and keynote speaker, she has appeared on CBS, Fox 26 News, on the cover of Business Today magazine, and a contributing writer for Huffington Post.

# BRIDGE LITERACY NOW

EMPOWERING WOMEN AND FAMILIES

Connie Rankin, a business owner, author of *God Gave Us Wings*, and founder of Bridge Literacy Now, a 501 (c) 3, firmly believes in the phrase "If Momma ain't happy, no one is happy!"

She knows firsthand how stressful life is for a child growing up in a poverty-stricken household with a single mother with little education, never knowing when they would be homeless. Sadly, this is the life in the U.S. of more than 39% of single moms with two children living in poverty. These moms spend half their incomes on rent and another one-third on childcare. This leaves little money for educational expenses and books.

Did you know-

- Two-thirds of students not reading by fourth-grade wind up in prison or on welfare.
- 70% of American prison inmates read below fourth-grade level.

Until the cycle of low literacy is broken, the cycle of poverty will remain unbroken, further entrenching the cradle-to-prison pipeline.

Bridge Literacy Now is collaborating with other non-profit organizations to help reclaim the future of America's fourth graders by donating books to women and their children. Our mission is to improve the quality of life for both moms and their children through education. Statistics show that enhancing a woman's education with a high school diploma or its equivalent could increase their income by 41% and improve the reading skills of their children. Therefore, weakening the cradle-to-prison pipeline and saving taxpayers an average of $44,000 per year for every child prevented from entering the criminal system.

Connie believes that Nelson Mandela says it best: "Education is the most powerful weapon which you can use to change the world."

She has committed to donating a portion of *God Gave Us Wings* book royalties to Bridge Literacy Now to provide educational seminars and books to ensure a better tomorrow for both moms and their fourth graders.

Your donation today will help reduce the prison population of the future.

Make your tax-deductible donations to
www.BridgeLiteracyNow.org.

# Morgan James
# Speakers Group

We connect Morgan James published authors with live and online events and audiences whom will benefit from their expertise.

Morgan James makes all of our titles available
through the Library for All Charity Organizations.

www.LibraryForAll.org